Creativity for a New Curriculum: 5–11

Creativity for a New Curriculum: 5–11 provides an account of what creativity really means in the context of children's learning in the primary school, and describes in practical terms what teachers can do to foster it. At a time of curriculum development and change, it focuses on the opportunity to build a new curriculum that is inclusive of creativity and is fit for the twenty-first century.

The value of fostering creative thinking and problem-solving abilities in education is widely recognized for its capacity to confer an independence and ability to function effectively in life. As such, encouraging children to be creative thinkers and problem solvers should be an integral part of everyday teaching and learning across all subjects.

Building upon the research and practices of a group of educators studying creativity across the curriculum and coordinated by the author, this book provides primary teachers and trainee teachers with easy to understand explanations of what creativity means in the context of the subjects of the curriculum for young children. It introduces ideas for how to nurture and support it, and explores issues associated with fostering it, such as assessment. Chapters cover areas including:

- A brief history of creativity and pedagogy, including common misconceptions
- Strategies for creative learning as well as creative teaching
- Creativity in English
- Creativity in Mathematics
- Creativity in Science and Design and Technology
- Creativity in Art and Music
- Creativity in History and the Humanities
- Creativity in ICT
- International perspectives on creativity

Creativity for a New Curriculum: 5–11 is an ideal source of information for teachers, teacher trainers, students on teaching programmes and anyone interested in developing opportunities for creativity across the primary school curriculum.

Lynn Newton is Professor of Education at Durham University, UK. She is Director of Initial Teacher Training and leads the primary sciences programmes. Previously she has worked in schools and has published widely in the areas of primary education and science and design and technology.

Creativity for a New Curriculum: 5–11

Edited by Lynn Newton

Routledge
Taylor & Francis Group

LONDON AND NEW YORK

First published 2012
by Routledge
2 Park Square, Milton Park, Abingdon, Oxon OX14 4RN

Simultaneously published in the USA and Canada
by Routledge
711 Third Avenue, New York, NY 10017

Routledge is an imprint of the Taylor & Francis Group, an informa business

British Library Cataloguing in Publication Data
A catalogue record for this book is available from the British Library

Library of Congress Cataloging in Publication Data
Creativity for a new curriculum: 5–11 / edited by Lynn D Newton.
    p. cm.
ISBN 978-0-415-61710-9 (hardback) – ISBN 978-0-415-61711-6 (paperback) –
ISBN 978-0-203-11771-2 (ebook) 1. Creative thinking–Study and teaching (Elementary)
2. Problem solving–Study and teaching (Elementary) 3. Curriculum change. I. Newton,
Lynn D., 1953-
LB1590.5.C75 2012
370.15'7–dc23   2012002379

ISBN: 978-0-415-61710-9 (hbk)
ISBN: 978-0-415-61711-6 (pbk)
ISBN: 978-0-203-11771-2 (ebk)

Typeset in Bembo
by Cenveo Publisher Services

Printed and bound in Great Britain by the MPG Books Group

Contents

About the Contributors

Anthony Blake joined the School of Education, Communication and Language Sciences in Newcastle University in May 2000, having worked as a teacher and deputy head teacher in primary schools in Newcastle and Gateshead from 1977. He has both an M.Litt. and Ed.D. from Newcastle University and is a Fellow of the Geological Society of London. As well as teaching on the Primary PGCE programme, he also runs undergraduate and postgraduate modules on the image of the teacher in popular culture and the representation of the past in British television drama. Current research activity is focused on the trainee teacher's understanding of creativity in primary school history and the role of film in supporting historical thinking by primary and secondary school-age students.

David Bolden is a lecturer in primary mathematics in the School of Education at Durham University where he teaches on both the PGCE Primary and the B.A. Primary Education programmes. His interest in mathematics began when he studied statistics at undergraduate level. He went on to teach statistics and mathematics in a number of further and higher education institutions before gaining his doctorate from Durham University. His thesis investigated primary teachers' epistemological views of the teaching and learning of mathematics. He has been involved in a number of projects related to the teaching and learning of mathematics. His research interests include creativity in mathematics, the role of representations in mathematical understanding, and teachers' epistemological views of mathematics.

Hazel Donkin teaches History of Art modules at Durham University and is a specialist in photography as an artistic medium. She also teaches an Arts option to undergraduate teacher trainees. With colleagues, she has recently been exploring some notions of artistic creativity amongst history of art students and how such notions are acquired through incidental learning. She is involved in a project with a group of artists exploring issues around speed in examinations and the relationship to thinking, well-being and identity.

Gail Edwards is a lecturer in the School of Education, Communication and Language Sciences in Newcastle University. She joined the university in 2003, having worked in primary schools in the North East region for several years. She currently teaches postgraduate education students. Her research interests are in the field of teacher education and its relation to social justice; in particular, her work examines the sociology of knowledge and its implications for teaching, curriculum and teacher education.

Alan Gleaves is a lecturer in ICT Education and Twenty-First Century Technologies in the School of Education, University of Durham. His research interests centre on ubiquitous learning with technology. Included under this umbrella are mobile devices, using blogs and electronic journals for reflective writing, and the formation of relational zones in online learning. Alan is also interested in the concepts of learner resilience and self-theory and how these can be addressed by new technologies. His recent work concerns how online novice teacher communities manage the experience of teaching practices when confronted with conflicting and complex emotions.

Dimitra Kokotsaki is a lecturer at the School of Education in Durham University where she runs the Postgraduate Certificate in secondary music education. She carries out research in music education across the primary and secondary school age range and is particularly interested in the educational and socio-psychological processes that operate in music making. She is currently completing a research project' funded by the Nuffield Foundation about improving the primary–secondary transition in music education in the North East of England and is currently the principal investigator in the evaluation of the *Restorative Approaches* initiative in County Durham. Her research interests include the identification and improvement of the educational, behavioural and socio-psychological conditions in schools with a specific focus on pupil creativity and engagement.

Douglas Newton teaches and researches in the School of Education at Durham University where he leads the Curriculum and Pedagogy Research Group. The group has a particular interest in creative thinking and the fostering of productive thought in the classroom in specific school subjects. He has published widely on various aspects of comprehension, understanding and creativity for teachers and researchers as well as on a range of educational issues, with over 30 books and 300 papers to his name. His successful book, *Teaching for Understanding: What it is and How to do it* (Routledge), is now available in an updated second edition which also relates understanding and creative thinking.

Lynn Newton is Divisional Director of Initial Teacher Training in the School of Education at Durham University. Previously, she worked in primary schools in the North of England, initially as a teacher and then as an advisory teacher for science and design-technology. After working at Newcastle University, she joined Durham University to lead the specialist primary science degree programme. Her research interests focus on effective communication, particularly the use of questions to promote understanding, and strategies that enhance learning in science. Her recent work has been in the area of creativity and she gave a keynote lecture on *Creativity and Productive Thought* at the 19th Biennial Conference of the *World Council for Gifted and Talented Children*, held in Prague in August 2011. She has published over a dozen books and over 100 research articles and papers, and spoken at a number of conferences.

Caroline Walker is Director for Undergraduate Education at Durham University and her research has two strands: first, it asks whether autobiographical approaches to teacher education can help to prepare more caring teachers, whose practices are characterized by relational fidelity and complex reflection. Caroline's other major research interest is in the educational achievements and social and emotional development of looked after children. She is particularly interested in how teachers frequently 'problematize' such children's abilities, and the ways in which they conceptualize fostered and adopted children's behaviours as narratives of difference and dysfunction.

Sophie Ward lectures in the School of Education at Durham University on matters relating to educational policy. She is an active member of the *Curriculum and Pedagogy* research group and has a particular interest in fostering creativity, self-awareness and social connectivity through drama. Her current work explores how creativity is believed to be perceived in different cultures and indicates some reservations about stereotypical notions.

David Waugh has published extensively on primary English. After a career in primary schools, including as a deputy head teacher, he directed primary PGCE at the University of Hull before becoming head of the education department there. In 2008, he became an adviser for initial teacher training for the government's National Strategies, working with universities across England on literacy, mathematics and inclusion. He also helped write several e-learning resources. He is currently course leader for the Primary PGCE programme at Durham University, where he is also responsible for English on the undergraduate ITT programme.

Introduction

Lynn Newton

This book is about fostering creativity and problem solving in the primary (or elementary) school classroom. It is for teachers and others interested in the education of primary aged pupils (5–11 years) who want to know more about what creativity means in the different areas of the curriculum usually taught to pupils of this age. Through an exploration of new and experienced teachers' understandings of what counts as creativity in different disciplines, we show that supporting creativity is not yet another experience to be added into an already over-crowded day. Rather, it is a way of thinking and working that can be developed and used in any subject area to enhance learning in that subject. Claxton, in his discussion about building learning power, argues that learning to learn has creativity at its heart (Claxton 2002: 5).

Creativity is a powerful capacity of human intelligence (Prentice 2000). It is also important. When supported and encouraged in classrooms it has been shown to improve motivation and self-esteem and raise achievement levels [Qualifications and Curriculum Authority (QCA) 2004]. However, it has been described as a complex and slippery concept (Prentice 2000; Philpott 2001). Even though it is valued, its underlying structures and perceived impact remain vague and elusive (Burnard 2006).

Anyone who has worked in education in the UK over the last 25 years will have experienced numerous challenges as various government initiatives have imposed themselves on teachers and their classroom practices. We have lived through the consequences of the 1986 Education Reform Act, which imposed a centrally controlled curriculum – the National Curriculum for 5–16-year-olds [see, e.g., Qualifications and Curriculum Development Agency (QCDA) 2011]. This has gone through several subsequent revisions since its introduction in 1989. Associated with this were programmes of study, attainment targets and standardized assessment tests at the ages of 7, 11 and 14 in English, maths and science. There has also been a rigorous model of accountability that emphasizes competition through league tables, rather than cooperation and collaboration between professionals. The debate about falling standards, particularly in literacy and numeracy, with constantly moving goal posts, international comparisons and targets to be met, have all added to the pressures on teachers. One consequence of the goal of raising standards was

1

the government-imposed strategies for literacy and numeracy. These were introduced at great expense only to be dropped by the current UK government following the May 2010 elections. Another initiative was the government-initiated review of the primary curriculum [the Rose Review; Department for Children, Schools and Families (DCSF) 2009] to guide the restructuring of the 'new' National Curriculum, again abandoned following the 2010 elections. This list could go on.

Nor are these challenges unique to England or the UK. For example, according to Baer and Garrett (2010), teachers in the USA are facing similar challenges, made more so because of the increasingly multicultural and multilingual population. They describe an unrelenting call for the raising of standards; standardized tests and more testing of students; the No Child Left Behind agenda; increasing visible teacher accountability; and the development of a Core Knowledge curriculum.

Whether in the UK or the USA, such challenges have consequences. There is plenty of research evidence that shows teachers feel a loss of control over the curriculum when they are told what to teach even if not how to teach it. This results in a lack of personal autonomy, freedom or flexibility. There is also evidence of pressure to teach for the standardized tests (that is, in the test year, teachers focus on preparing children for the tests). Also, in the push to meet targets (for reading and numeracy levels in particular) there is little time left to do the 'value added' bits – the 'extras' they want to do. One particular 'extra' that is lost is the freedom to spend time teaching for creativity.

For well over a decade, educators and policy makers in countries around the world have been urging creativity in our schools, from creative teaching to stimulate interest and to motivate pupils to creative outcomes in the form of creative and critical thinking and problem solving on the part of the learners. In England, the general requirements of the National Curriculum [Department for Education and Employment (DfEE)/QCA 1999) identified six key skill areas, one of which was helping learners to improve their own learning performance. Within this skill area, developing thinking skills and problem-solving abilities is seen as crucial. Thinking skills incorporate information processing, reasoning, enquiry, creativity and evaluation. In particular, learners need opportunities to explore different kinds of:

- creative thinking, for example, amending or adapting an idea, creating and using analogies, designing new ways to do something;
- critical thinking, for example, introducing concepts of evidence in science, validating and justifying choices in design and technology (D&T), testing assumptions in history'; and
- problem solving – raising questions and searching for answers drawing on existing and new ideas and information, generating alternative possibilities, and choosing from the options with reasons, evaluating outcomes against criteria.

Moore (2008) argues that research findings indicate that when such thinking skills are an integral part of the curriculum and instructional practice, test scores improve. He suggests therefore that 'teachers of every discipline must teach thinking skills explicitly in addition to their content area' (Moore 2008: 313). However, to do this requires teachers who are not only very secure in both the skills, knowledge and understandings that underpin the different subject disciplines, but also know what counts as creativity in the different disciplines.

The UK government's primary national strategy document, *Excellence and Enjoyment*, stated that in order to meet the needs of the twenty-first century, schools must nurture a creative curriculum that would develop students' capacities for original ideas and actions [Department for Education and Skills (DfES) 2003: 2]. Around the same time, in response to a national debate on the education of 3–18-year-olds, the Scottish Executive produced *A Curriculum for Excellence* [Scottish Executive Education Department (SEED) 2004]. This focused on one of the National Priorities, which was to enable pupils to 'think creatively and independently' and so become successful learners [Her Majesty's Inspectors – Education (HMIe) 2006]. Nor is this interest in encouraging creative thinking unique to the UK. An interest in fostering creativity is also to be seen in policy documents from, for example, Australia, Cyprus, Japan, Korea, New Zealand, Singapore, and the USA (American Association for the Advancement of Science 1990; Schwartz-Geschka 1994; Ritchie and Edwards 1996; Diakidoy and Kanari 1999; Tan 2000; Park *et al.* 2006; Milne 2007). Perceptions of the desirability of creativity, however, depend on the culture and may not be encouraged in the classroom (Kwang 2001).

The Scottish Executive report mentioned earlier (SEED 2004) also noted that, while teachers were enthusiastic about the principles enabling the pupils to think creatively and independently, they were less certain about the implementation and the practice. Teachers were, generally, confident about teaching creatively, with an abundance of ideas to stimulate interest and ability to plan accordingly. This is hardly surprising. As Penny *et al.* (2002: 25) point out, 'Creativity is … a necessary part of all teaching'. This focuses on the creativity in teaching but meaningful and appropriate learning activities that interest the children do not necessarily mean that the children themselves are being creative. The Scottish Executive report found that the teachers were less certain about teaching *for* creativity – encouraging creative thinking on the part of the learners themselves. This uncertainty has been noted in teachers in other countries, working with learners of varying age and across a range of subject disciplines. Teachers also struggle with how to recognize and evaluate creativity and how to assess their own success at promoting it. Behind such uncertainty lie a number of central questions. What does creativity mean? Can all pupils be creative? Is it possible to be creative in all subjects? How can teachers promote creative thinking in the pupils they teach? How can its quality be evaluated to inform teaching? It is a response to these kinds of questions that this book hopes to provide.

The emphasis in the book is on teaching for creativity rather than teaching creatively. The focus is on the creative learner not the creative teacher. Jeffrey (2006: 407), in his study of creative teaching and learning in classrooms in nine European countries, describes creative learning as being innovative, experimental, inventive and involving knowledge enquiry to solve problems. He describes this as possibility thinking and engagement with problems.

We work on the premise that all pupils can be creative to some degree, from the pre-school or early years children to the older primary school child at the sharp end of centrally controlled curricula and narrow assessment procedures, where the opportunity to problem solve, take risks in their learning decisions, and think creatively might not be evident. We describe notions of creativity in thought and actions in different subject disciplines and illustrate how important the interaction between skills, knowledge, understanding and experience are for developing deeper and more meaningful learning.

Colleagues in the *Curriculum and Pedagogy Research Group* in the School of Education of Durham University have been exploring for several years what counts as creativity in different subject disciplines. Through work with teachers, both those in training and experienced teachers working in schools, they have explored notions of creativity in the different disciplines. This book is a synthesis of that work to provide an overview of their findings, embedding it in the wider context of research and practice from around the world, and making some recommendations for action in primary classrooms.

In Chapter 1, Douglas Newton sets the scene for the subsequent chapters. He explores reasons why creativity is important and provides an overview of creative thinking and problem solving in the context of education and schooling. After a brief review of research on the concept of creativity and the problem of definitions, he discusses current views of children as creative individuals. He introduces the polymorphic nature of creativity and explores popular conceptions of the creative enterprise and the importance of knowing what it is.

The next three chapters focus on those subjects at the heart of most curricula: a language, mathematics and science. An account of what creative thinking can mean for children in primary English is introduced in Chapter 2 by Lynn Newton and David Waugh. Common conceptions of creativity and problem solving in the context of a language and the implications of mismatches are considered. Ways to foster creative thinking in English are suggested and illustrated. In Chapter 3, David Bolden provides an account of what creative thinking can mean for children in primary school mathematics and contrasts this with mathematical algorithmic problem solving. Common conceptions of creativity in mathematics are described and the implications of mismatches are considered. Strategies for fostering creativity in mathematics are described and illustrated. An account of what creative thinking and problem solving can mean for children in primary science is provided by Lynn Newton in Chapter 4. She relates the discussion to creativity and problem solving in design and technology, an area of the curriculum that, as the chapter illustrates, is closely related to science. It is often considered to be the problem-solving dimension commonly called the 'appliance of science'.

An account of what creative thinking can mean for children in other primary curricular areas is discussed in the next block of chapters. Art and music are discussed by Douglas Newton, Hazel Donkin, Dimitra Kokotsaki and Lynn Newton in Chapter 5. Both areas are traditionally associated with creative outcomes, and the team discuss conceptions of the creative artist and observer, and the creative composer, musician and listener. Teachers' common conceptions of what it means to be creative in these contexts in the primary classroom are discussed, some of which may be remnants from past conceptions. Nevertheless, they shape thought about these and other subjects. How to foster creativity in art and music is explored with some strategies for practice being described and illustrated. Representing the humanities, Anthony Blake and Gail Edwards discuss history and geography in Chapter 6. An account of what creative thinking can mean for children in primary school history and geography is considered, and what teaching for creativity means in these contexts is explored and exemplified through the work done with student teachers in Newcastle University. Fostering creative thinking in history and geography through some suggested strategies is described and illustrated.

Information and communications technology (ICT) can be viewed as both a subject and as a tool or skill. This presents challenges when thinking about creativity, some of which are discussed by Caroline Walker and Alan Gleaves in Chapter 7. An account of what creative thinking can mean for children in primary ICT is followed by some suggestions for fostering creative thinking in ICT. Usefully, many of the strategies are cross-curricular, and can be applied more widely.

The problem of recognizing and assessing creative processes and products is the focus of Chapter 8, where Douglas Newton explores the difficult question of whether or not children's creativity can be assessed. He seeks to understand the assessment of creativity through his 'Insider–Outsider' model, which can be used as a means of informing teaching rather than making summative judgements of children. How creativity is seen in education more globally is explored by Sophie Ward and Lynn Newton in Chapter 9. Some of the stereotypical ideas about creativity in education worldwide are presented and challenged, some dilemmas introduced, particularly in connection with East–West perspectives, and some similarities and differences discussed. In the final chapter, Chapter 10, Lynn Newton draws together some of the ideas from the earlier chapters and identifies some tensions and opportunities.

References

American Association for the Advancement of Science (AAAS) (1990) *Project 2061: Science for All Americans*, New York: Oxford University Press.

Baer, J. and Garrett, T. (2010) 'Teaching for creativity in an era of content standards', Ch. 2, pp. 6–23, in R.A. Beghetto and J.C. Kaufman (eds) *Nurturing Creativity in the Classroom*, Cambridge: Cambridge University Press.

Burnard, P. (2006) 'Reflecting on the creativity agenda in education', *Cambridge Journal of Education*, 36(3): 313–18.

Claxton, G. (2002) *Building Learning Power: Helping Young People Become Better Learners*, Bristol: TLO.

Department for Children, Schools and Families (DCSF) (2009) *Independent Review of the Primary Curriculum* (the Rose Review). Online. Available at: http://www.education.gov.uk/publications/Primary_curriculum-report.pdf (accessed 19 January 2011).

Department for Education and Employment/Qualifications and Curriculum Authority (DfEE/QCA) (1999) *The National Curriculum Handbook for Primary Teachers in England Key Stages 1 and 2*, London: DfEE/QCA.

Department for Education and Skills (DfES) (2003) *Excellence and Enjoyment: A Strategy for Primary Schools*, Nottingham: DfES Publications Centre.

Diakidoy, I.A.N. and Kanari, E. (1999) 'Student teachers' beliefs about creativity', *British Educational Research Journal*, 25(2): 225–43.

Her Majesty's Inspectors – Education (HMIe) (2006) *Emerging Good Practice in Promoting Creativity: a report by HMIE*, March. Available at: www.hmie.gov.uk/documents/publication/hmiepcie.html.

Jeffrey, B. (2006) 'Creative teaching and learning: towards a common discourse and practice', *Cambridge Journal of Education*, 36(3): 399–414.

Kwang, N.A. (2001) *Why Asians are Less Creative than Westerners*, Singapore: Prentice-Hall.

Milne, I. (2007) 'Children's science', *Primary Science Review*, 100: 33–4.

Moore, K.D. (2008) *Effective Instructional Strategies from Theory to Practice*, London: Sage Publications.

Park, S., Soo-Young, L., Oliver, S. and Cramond, B. (2006) 'Changes in Korean science teachers' perceptions of creativity and science teaching after participating in an overseas professional development program', *Journal of Science Teacher Education*, 17(1): 37–64.

Penny, S., Ford, R., Price, L. and Young, S. (2002) *Teaching Arts in Primary Schools*, Exeter: Learning Matters.

Philpott, C. (2001) *Learning to Teach Music in the Secondary School*, London: RoutledgeFalmer.

Prentice, R. (2000) 'Creativity: a reaffirmation of its place in early childhood education', *The Curriculum Journal*, 11(2): 145–58.

Qualifications and Curriculum Authority (QCA) (2004) *Creativity: Find It, Promote It! Promoting pupils' creative behaviour across the curriculum at key stages 1, 2 and 3 – Practical materials for schools*, Sudbury, Suffolk: QCA Publications.

Qualifications and Curriculum Development Agency (QCDA) (2011) *National Curriculum: Key Stages 1 and 2*. Online. Available at: http://curriculum.qcda.gov.uk/key-stages-1-and-2/subjects/ (accessed 3 August 2011).

Ritchie, S.M. and Edwards, J. (1996) 'Creative thinking instruction for aboriginal children', *Learning and Instruction*, 6(1): 59–75.

Schwartz-Geschka, M. (1994) 'Creativity in Japanese society', *Creativity and Innovation Management*, 3(4): 229–32.

Scottish Executive Education Department (SEED) (2004) *A Curriculum for Excellence*. Online. Available at: http://www.acurriculumforexcellencescotland.gov.uk/ (accessed 10 July 2010).

Tan, A.G. (2000) 'A review of the study of creativity in Singapore', *Journal of Creative Behavior*, 34(4): 259–84.

Creativity and Problem Solving: An Overview

Douglas Newton

In the beginning

Some 40,000 years ago, stemming from developing abilities in speech, there was an explosion in people's creativity. It showed itself in, for instance, story-telling, art, artefacts, personal ornaments, and religion-making. Being creative and able to solve problems is a decided advantage in a potentially fragile existence. It is not just new ideas and objects which make a difference but new ways of doing things, of orchestrating actions and of seeing the world, which increase the likelihood of survival. This creative ability has been described as one of the most striking features of our species and something which marks us off from others. As then, so it is now: children explore, practise and develop their creative abilities through imaginative, pretend play in preparation for adult life when, if they are disposed to use it, it can be a valuable asset (Carruthers 2002; MacWhinney 2005; Miller 2000).

While creative ability and the disposition to use it vary from person to person, it is neither the unique possession of a few, special, gifted people nor is it confined to particular areas of activity (Prentice 2000). Nor does the act have to produce something of great novelty or significance to the world to be creative. We are all creative from time to time as when we solve the problems of everyday life. And included in this are children who, like adults, are being creative when they make or think of something which is new *to them* (Thurstone 1952).

The notion of creativity

Historically, poets were the ones who were considered to be creative. Artists, popularly seen today as the archetypes of creative people, were thought of as artisans who copied or mimicked what they saw; they did not bring something into the world that had not existed before in some form. But, by the nineteenth century, notions of creativity widened and it was accepted that artists could do more than replicate the world.

Those engaged in what became known as the 'creative arts' of music, drama and dance followed them into the fold but the word 'creative' was generally not applied to other areas, like mathematics, science, geography and history, until relatively recently. Now, it is generally accepted that most areas of human endeavour offer opportunities for creation (Tatarkiewicz 1980; Euster 1987; Treffinger *et al.* 2002). Why has this taken so long? Surely, coming up with bright ideas is what people do in any endeavour. Isn't the kind of thought which goes into it much the same? The problem is that the bright ideas may not look the same or be called the same thing in the diverse areas of human activity. To see what they share, we need to be above the differences and look down.

Creativity has been described in many ways but a common theme today is that it is a personal activity intent on producing something new. For instance, it is a 'performance where the individual is producing something new and unpredictable' (Bergström 1984: 159, cited in Pehkonen 1997). 'New' here has a broad meaning. It obviously includes, for instance, novel artefacts and ideas and new ways of working, but it also includes the ways in which things and ideas are brought together to produce a desired effect. For example, while we might create a new word, a new colour or a new idea, we can also be creative in how we use existing words, existing colours, and existing ideas to produce the effects we want. As Carruthers (2002: 227) points out, 'anyone who is imagining how things could be other than they are will be thinking creatively', so what it takes is imagination. But simply being imaginative is not enough: it is not a case of anything goes, 'having fun and coming up with wacky ideas' (Howe 2004: 15), 'doing your own thing' (Fisher 1990: 33) or 'fun and free expression' (Gouge and Yates 2002: 137). Being creative needs 'mental discipline, prior experience and knowledge'. Sternberg (2006) has pointed out that the process is, in essence, one of taking decisions, conscious and unconscious, about what to do. For instance, the artist, Henri Matisse, appeared to paint in a continuous flow but slow-motion film showed that, before each stroke of the brush, he hesitated. In that short interval and perhaps largely unconsciously, he considered various possibilities then chose one he felt was appropriate (Merleau-Ponty 1964).

Crucially, there has also to be some form of quality control so that what is produced is appropriate, it does what was intended and achieves its goal (Gouge and Yates 2002: 137). In the UK, the National Advisory Committee on Creative and Cultural Education (NACCCE) caught this well in its definition of creativity as an 'imaginative activity fashioned so as to produce outcomes that are both original and of value' (NACCCE 1999). The artist, the historian and the engineer may all strive to produce what is appropriate, effective, functional or fitting, but this reference to value, broadly defined, points to an implicit social aspect of creativity: it is, in the final analysis, others who evaluate and validate the product (Csikszentmihalyi 1996).

To these essential attributes have been added some that are desirable. For instance, a creative product is seen as better if it is elegant, well-crafted, or economical (Besemer and O'Quin 1987, 1999). An economically short, mathematical proof is likely to be seen as preferable to a long, convoluted one that achieves the same end, all else being equal. Cropley (2001) adds that creative activity should be ethical and Craft (2008) points out it should be wisely used. Ethics refers to what people generally agree are right and wrong behaviours. For instance, is it ethical to make people feel a need for a new product which is no better than what already exists? Wisdom is broader and gives due consideration to the contextual matters, material and people touched by the situation. For instance, although the product is no better than what exists and making it may add carbon dioxide to the atmosphere, selling it would keep people in employment.

The past, however, is in the present, and popular conceptions of creativity and creative people are often coloured by stereotypes drawn from the arts and stories of exceptionally gifted people's creativity and inventiveness (Prentice 2000; Claxton *et al.* 2006). Because of this, many would deny that they are creative and have even been creative today.

Why is there an interest in creativity?

Piaget believed that the principal goal of education is to produce creative people (Fisher 1990) and, from a philosophical point of view, it can be argued that, 'A meaningful life is a creative one' (Taylor 1999: 9). Life presents us with problems, large and small, often unlike what we have met before. I recall a garden shed which needed a flexible drainpipe to collect the water from the roof. The gardener's solution was to use some plastic bottles cut into short tubes and inserted one inside another to make a pipe which led to the water butt. In someone's kitchen, I noticed that a length of elastic cord with hooks on the ends discreetly prevented a trolley tray from tipping when loaded unevenly. People with a creative disposition will generally cope in new situations when problems like these present themselves. Those without it have to accept inefficiency, inconvenience and the status quo or rely on others to solve problems for them. The ability and disposition to be creative offers a valuable kind of autonomy and personal effectiveness which can be empowering, satisfying and fulfilling. In the UK, this has led to creativity being described as a thinking, key or life skill [Qualifications and Curriculum Authority (QCA) 2005; Department for Education and Skills (DfES) 2006; Scottish Executive Education Department (SEED) 2006]. But, beyond this everyday value of creativity is also, in the long term, the possibility of worthwhile contributions to culture (NACCCE 1999; Craft 2002). For the politician, on the other hand, creative people can contribute to an economy through the 'creative industries', such as, design, fashion, software production, marketing, advertising, pop music, the performing arts, publishing, new technologies, and research and development (Osborne 2003). Beghetto (2007: 1) argues that creativity is 'The ultimate economic resource and an essential for addressing complex individual and societal issues'. Schools, however, may not do much to foster creativity, at least in the form of constrained, purposeful imagination across the curriculum. Instead, they have tended to favour memory and analytical thought (Fisher 1990; Craft 2002; Sternberg 2006; Garner 2007). The Plowden Report [Central Advisory Council for Education (England) (CACE) 1967] argued for activities to foster imagination, largely through play, but this tended to be interpreted as encouraging artistic novelty without regard for what was worthwhile – anything that was different was considered to be 'good' (Barrow and Woods 1975). Now, teachers are urged to foster creativity and problem-solving skills across the curriculum (Craft 2002; DfES 2003; SEED 2006). Attendant advantages are brought to their attention, such as the way creative activities have been found to improve behaviour, social skills, self-esteem, motivation and achievement [QCA 2005; Office for Standards in Education (Ofsted) 2006]. Creative activity can also be a useful way of providing for the learning needs of more able learners and for those who are socially, emotionally and behaviourally disturbed (Massey and Burnard 2006; Haydon 2008). Interest in fostering creativity in the classroom is widespread [see, for instance, American Association for the Advancement of Science (AAAS) 1990; Schwartz-Geschka 1994; Ritchie and Edwards 1996; Diakidoy and Kanari 1999; Tan 2000; Park *et al.* 2006]. In short, fostering creativity is said to be good for the economy, society, communities, education and the individual, at least in the West (Burnard and White 2008).

Not everyone, however, sees encouraging creativity as entirely good. McLaren (1999) has argued that perpetual innovation threatens a society's stability and cohesion and risks producing anxious, uneasy people. Osborne (2003) believes that the doctrine of creativity has achieved the status of an unwarranted virtue. The pursuit of creativity, he contends, has become a moral imperative endowed with an unwarranted intrinsic value and romantic connotations of inspiration and heroism. Certainly, highly successful creators can become household names, quite literally. A vacuum cleaner doesn't vacuum the carpet but 'hoovers' it (and perhaps will have to become '"dysons" it'). It all lends a spurious morality to convincing people to accept 'the cult of the new', that change *per se* is worthwhile and that they have needs when they do not. Craft (2003) asks if we should encourage a throw-away society; although good for the economy, it could be bad for the environment and waste resources. She also asks if we should not, instead, foster a 'make-do-and-mend' attitude. Just because something is possible does not mean it must become reality. She argues for ethics and wisdom when bringing something new into the world and suggests we think carefully before imposing Western values on societies where individual creativity is not so highly valued (Craft 2006).

These are serious concerns about the kind of society we could produce and it would be irresponsible to foster creativity blindly. But teaching young children is not about preparing them for some specific place in the labour market: it is about equipping them with what they need to lead fulfilled lives and be discerning members of society. Being able and disposed to be creative when it is needed has the potential to point children in the direction which could lead to such lives. It equips them to deal with everyday problems and have the potential to thrive, at least on an individual and family scale, avoiding what Best (1982: 292–3) has called 'vegetating apathy'. Even a 'make-do-and-mend' society calls for a high level of creativity to do the making and mending. Meanwhile, in the classroom, while practising thinking creatively, there is the opportunity for children to consider the value of specific products: just because it is new does not mean it is better or that we need it; we have choices and choices have consequences. Piaget's (1932) work has suggested that this kind of thought can be too advanced for children but, although they may not be able to draw major generalizations and deal in abstractions, it is likely that they will be able to engage with an understandable issue in local and familiar contexts, albeit without the depth of critical thought we expect of an adult (Baltes and Staudinger 2000). Craft (2006) has suggested that fostering creativity with wisdom in this way could help to nurture a child's moral development.

On balance, then, we see fostering creative thinking in children as a worthwhile goal. An imaginative resourcefulness can support diverse activities from creative communication to ingenuity in solving practical problems. It has the potential to develop in children an autonomy of thought and action which could support them in adulthood. Furthermore, exercising creativity in the classroom offers opportunities to demythologize the activity and to subject it and its products to critical thought. Excluding it from formal education risks leaving it to chance, could deprive children of a valuable capability, and leaves them dependent on others for both creativity and its evaluation. At the instrumental level in the classroom, creative activities can be rewarding, motivating and engaging for learners in general and provide an effective means of personalizing learning for the gifted and talented (Newton and Newton 2010). In other words, such activity adds to a teacher's store of tools for fostering learning.

Children being creative

Can children be creative? Scholars like Ausubel (1978) and Csikszentmihalyi (1996), saw children as incapable of producing something new and appropriate to the world. They simply do not have the knowledge and know-how. Nevertheless, while they may not produce something new to the world, Williams (1970) and Petty (1997) point out that children can create something new, at least *to themselves* and new to others like themselves. This 'new to the person' perspective has been called psychological or 'little c' creativity (Richards 1993; Gardner 1993; Boden 1996). So, for instance, a child might create a plausible account of an event in history, a way of decorating writing paper to make a gift, or an experiment to test a tentative explanation in science. They may not be new to the teacher or to any other adult. Indeed, they are likely to be able to do better themselves but, in the child's world, they are new. Often, adults engage in little c creativity, too. It is less stringent than the 'new to the world' requirement which has been called historical creativity or the 'big C' view. The point is that children can be creative and, in the process, they have the opportunity to practise and develop their creative thinking skills.

Creative thinking is not necessarily different from kinds of thinking we use on a more or less daily basis (Amabile 1983; Boden 2004). For instance, when we understand something we make mental connections between ideas and, hence, construct coherent, meaningful wholes. The point is that *we* create those mental connections. In other words, constructing an understanding is essentially a personal, creative process and what we produce is often new to us (Newton 2011). We are born with the ability to construct such understandings; being able to make sense of the world has survival value (Mithen 1996; Wolpert 2003). Most of the time, what we construct like this is much like what others construct; in other words, our understandings are similar enough to say we share them. On occasions, however, we may make connections which produce an understanding which is new to the world. In the classroom, what a child constructs with our help is likely to be new to the child (why else would we do it?). If we helped the child a lot, we tend not to see it as being creative. Instead, we tend to reserve the word for those occasions when a child constructs an understanding more or less unaided. For example, a child asked to explain why a torch bulb wired to a battery on a table has not lit up might make sense of it by making a connection between the flow of water in a pipe and electricity in a wire. Accordingly, she says that the battery needs to be lifted higher so that the electricity can run down to the bulb. The point is that this understanding was constructed (created) by the child and, while it is not the accepted understanding, it has some plausibility in the world of the child. In short, the child has been creative in producing an explanation, novel to the child, which could be put to the test.

Moseley *et al.* (2005) prefer to describe such creative thinking as productive thought. Productive thought includes reasoning, understanding, systematic enquiry, problem solving and creative thinking. Psychological tests may show that some children are, indeed, better at productive thought than others but productive thought is not the preserve of a gifted few. Everyone may possess the ability to some degree and the teacher's role is to bring it out and increase a willingness to use it.

Creative thinking and problem solving

While there may be a family likeness between productive thought in, say, science, history and art, there are also differences, just as in a family. In science, thought constructs causal explanations, in history it puts together plausible motives, and in art, it finds ways of communicating ideas and feelings (Seefeldt 1995; Newton 2011). While creative thought in various subjects may have something in common, each has its own flavour (Claxton 2006). Furthermore, not only does the content differ but so do the kinds of constraint placed on imagination. Imagination produces the ideas and critical thought constrains them. When artists were asked to rate originality (e.g. novel, unusual) appropriateness (e.g. function, plausible) and impression (e.g. elegance, attractiveness) for their importance in their work, they valued novelty and impression more than appropriateness. When architects were asked to do the same, they rated appropriateness more highly than the others (Glück *et al.* 2002). We asked scientists for their evaluations and they gave each roughly equal weighting. For an architect, a building must stand up, be functional, safe and satisfy the brief. The others are irrelevant if function is not satisfied. The artist is often not so tightly bound so, presumably, is a little less concerned with it. Scientists, on the other hand, seem to want to give equal attention to all these, perhaps because novel, plausible and elegant science stands more chance of being published and accepted.

Problem solving and creativity

In domains like science, strongly constrained productive thought tends to be called problem solving. That which seems (at least to the outside world) as less constrained, tends to be called creativity (Maker *et al.* 2008). Although the words are different, the thought is still creative. For instance, composing music is generally seen as a creative activity *par excellence* yet the task can be described as problem solving, even by a composer (Newton and Newton 2006) The problem might be how to create a piece of for a particular occasion. The composer, Harvey, has described such problems as stimulating and challenging (Harvey 1999).

Although creativity in various domains may bear a family resemblance, differences matter. It would be wrong to foster productive thought in say, history, which was not historically plausible or in technology which was not technologically functional. While it might be easier to maintain distinctions when subjects are taught separately, they may be taught together in a more or less integrated or cross-curricular way in the primary school. On such occasions, a teacher needs a clear notion of creativity in general and creativity and problem solving in particular subjects. Their conceptions of creativity in school subjects may affect what they do, their classroom climate, and what they value and reward (Fernstermacher and Soltis 1986; Baer 1997; Esquivel 1995).

Conceptions of creativity

On the one hand, as Osborne (2003) has pointed out, people can have romantic images of the creative process as eureka moments of inspiration in which something new to the world somehow suddenly comes into being. In reality, the process is often, even usually, very different. Cézanne, for instance, insisted that art was not inspired but simply very hard work while for Edison invention was 10 per cent inspiration and 90 per cent perspiration. Creativity is also routinely attached to that area of activity commonly called the arts, hence, 'the creative arts'. At least to my knowledge we never see reference to 'the creative sciences' or 'the creative humanities'. Although imagination is often seen to be involved in creativity, someone who successfully follows detailed instructions to make something may also be called creative. For example, someone who knits a sweater closely following a pattern may produce a very attractive garment and may be described as creative. Without dismissing the value of the activity, the word is reserved for those occasions where the activity is less productive. In everyday usage, 'to create' can have connotations of 'to make'. At the same time, some cultures may not encourage creative behaviour, seeing it as something which marks people out as different and not conforming to the culture's norms (Kwang 2001; Runco and Johnson 2002). Children may similarly not admire creativity in their peers so those who have creative thoughts and actions may conceal them to avoid persecution (Torrance 1975).

Against this background, Western teachers generally see being creative as producing something novel, largely epitomized by artistic creativity (e.g. Dickinson *et al.* 2000; Davies *et al.* 2004, Edmonds 2004). They may even believe they support creative thought in their classrooms but, in reality, provide little opportunity for it (Aljughaiman and Mowrer-Reynolds 2005; Cropley 2001). Other teachers believe the fostering of creative thought is irrelevant in their classes (Kennedy 2005). This is particularly evident in subjects like mathematics where the acquisition of established procedures or algorithms is seen as paramount. In such situations, creative thinking can be an unwanted distraction from the purpose of the lesson (Beghetto 2007).

But, even when teachers have conceptions of creativity which broadly accord with definitions such as that of the NACCCE (1999), this does not mean that what they do in the classroom supports creativity in a given context. Painting something adequately with a broad brush does not mean that the fine detail of what should happen in particular subjects underlies it. Teachers' conceptions of creativity in a particular subject could be a combination of their conceptions of creativity in general and their conceptions of that particular subject (for combined conceptions, see Costello and Keane 1992). Consider the problem of creativity in geography if someone's conception of creativity in general stemmed from what it is in art and conception of geography amounted to learning the names of cities, capes and bays. What would they see as appropriate? Would it be the making of aesthetically pleasing, accurate maps? Putting aside such a caricature, limitations in either conception are likely to make themselves felt in the combination.

Only by knowing something of teachers' conceptions as they relate to the teaching of specific subjects can we approach what they might do in the classroom (e.g. Fryer and Collings 1991; Brickhouse and Bodner 1992; Waters-Adams 2006). Even then, the link between teachers' general conceptions and what they do in the classroom is not always simple or direct. But, while a teacher may know what creativity means in the classroom and be unable or unwilling to give time to it, a teacher who does *not* know what it means is unlikely to support it well even if they want to do so or believe they do. In short, we believe that teachers need some grasp of what 'children being creative' means in each of the subjects they must teach.

Teaching for creativity

Traditionally, schools have been about passing on the known (Illich 1971). Teaching about the possible – particularly when children are to do the possibility thinking themselves – is less certain, outcomes are more open and events less determined. Generally, it involves encouraging imaginative thought, allowing space and time for children to question, explore and manipulate ideas, gently drawing attention to constraints and cautiously intervening to maintain productive thought and safety. Cremin *et al.* (2006) describe the teacher's role in this as the 'permission giver', permission to do, to try, to explore, to change and to produce. Maker *et al.* (2008) recommend active learning, providing choices, a ready access to materials to work with and time for exploration. Grainger and Barnes (2006), commenting on the kind of environment which fosters creativity, suggest it should be active but relaxed, supportive, serious but with a touch of playfulness, and offer a mix of individual and cooperative activity. Wegerif (2010) argues for dialogue between teacher and learner, and learner and learner so that problems are solved collaboratively. The teacher models creative activity, encourages children to ask 'What if?' questions, guiding them to productive thought and, later, helping them apply their successful approaches to new problems. From advice like this and elsewhere (e.g. Harrington 1990), it seems worthwhile to:

- try to develop a creative atmosphere through stories, displays and talk;
- find open-ended tasks which the children find relevant and meaningful;
- help the children to understand the task and, if necessary, draw out ideas from them to show what might be possible;
- arrange for periods of dialogue interspersed with periods of private reflection;
- provide opportunities and time for children to explore ideas and materials they will use, even if it looks like play;
- build up a collection of safe, accessible resources and information, and deliberately include some that are unusual, funny or otherwise different from the norm;
- think about your own role as teacher, guide and role model;

- encourage children to try out their ideas and evaluate them themselves;
- consider safety always and retain your role as permission giver.

Shallcross (1981), on the other hand, suggests what to avoid. For example:

- do not have one 'correct' outcome or solution to a problem in your mind;
- do not expect the children to simply get on with it;
- avoid overly limited and limiting resources; and
- do not allow children's ideas to be ridiculed – make it clear that many ideas fail.

When children are not used to opportunities for creative activity, they may not know how to handle the freedom of thought and action or the dialogue and private reflection, so more structure may be needed intiatially. Furthermore, developing children's dispositions to be creative can take time. It helps if the enterprise is school-wide, with everyone working towards the same goal. Later chapters will interpret and illustrate the above advice in specific subject contexts. While there may be some enthusiasm for fostering creative thought in a school, it also has to be remembered it is not something which is needed all the time and that variety is the spice of life.

References

Aljughaiman, A. and Mowrer-Reynolds, E. (2005) 'Teachers' conceptions of creativity and creative students', *Journal of Creative Behavior*, 39(1): 17–34.

Amabile, T.M. (1983) *The Social Psychology of Creativity*, New York: Springer-Verlag.

American Association for the Advancement of Science (AAAS) (1990) *Project 2061: Science for All Americans*, New York: Oxford University Press.

Ausubel, D.P. (1978) *Educational Psychology*, New York: Holt, Rinehart and Winston.

Baer, J. (1997) *Creative Teachers, Creative Students*, Boston, MA: Allyn and Bacon.

Baltes, P.B. and Staudinger, U.M. (2000) 'Wisdom', *American Psychologist*, 55: 122–36.

Barrow, R. and Woods, R. (1975) *An Introduction to Philosophy of Science*, London: Methuen.

Beghetto, R.A. (2007) 'Does creativity have a place in classroom discussions? Teachers' response preferences', *Thinking Skills and Creativity*, 2(1): 1–9.

Besemer, S.P. and O'Quin, K. (1987) 'Creative product analysis', in S.G. Isaksen (ed.) *Frontiers of Creativity Research*, Buffalo: Bearly.

Besemer, S.P. and O'Quin, K. (1999) 'Confirming the three-factor creative product analysis matrix model in an American sample', *Creativity Research Journal*, 12(4): 287–96.

Best, D. (1982) 'Can creativity be taught?', *British Journal of Educational Studies*, 30(3): 280–94.

Boden, M.A. (1996) 'What is creativity?' in M.A. Boden (ed.) *Dimensions of Creativity*, Cambridge, MA: Massachusetts Institute of Technology.

Boden, M.A. (2004) *The Creative Mind – Myths and Mechanisms*, London: Routledge.

Brickhouse, N. and Bodner, G.M. (1992) 'The beginning science teacher: classroom narratives of conviction and constraints', *Journal of Research in Science Teaching*, 29(5): 471–85.

Burnard, P. and White, J. (2008) 'Creativity and performativity', *British Educational Research Journal*, 34(5): 667–82.

Central Advisory Council for Education (England) (CACE) (1967) *Children and their Primary Schools (The Plowden Report)*, London: HMSO.

Carruthers, P. (2002) 'Human creativity', *British Journal of the Philosophy of Science*, 53: 225–49.

Claxton, G. (2006) 'Thinking at the edge: soft creativity', *Cambridge Journal of Education*, 36(3), 351–62.

Claxton, G., Edwards, L., and Scale-Constantinou, V. (2006) 'Cultivating creative mentalities', *Thinking Skills and Creativity*, 1: 57–61.

Costello, F. and Keane, M.T. (1992) 'Concept combination: a theoretical review', *Irish Journal of Psychology*, 13: 125–40.

Craft, A. (2002) *Creativity and Early Years Education*, London: Continuum.

Craft, A. (2003) 'The limits to creativity in education: dilemmas for the educator', *British Journal of Educational Studies*, 51(2): 113–27.

Craft, A. (2006) 'Fostering creativity with wisdom', *Cambridge Journal of Education*, 36(3): 337–50.

Craft, A. (2008) 'Nurturing creativity, wisdom, and trusteeship in education', in A. Craft, H. Gardner and G. Claxton (eds) *Creativity, Wisdom and Trusteeship*, Thousand Oaks: Corwin.

Cremin, T., Burnard, P. and Craft, A. (2006) 'Pedagogy and possibility thinking in the early years', *Thinking Skills and Creativity*, 1: 108–19.

Cropley, A.J. (2001) *Creativity in Education and Learning*, London: Kogan Page.

Csikszentmihalyi, M. (1996) *Creativity: Flow and the Psychology of Discovery and Invention*, New York: HarperCollins.

Davies, D., Howe, A., Rogers, M. and Fasciato, M. (2004) 'How do trainee primary teachers understand creativity?' in E. Norman, D. Spendlove, P. Graver and A. Mitchell (eds) *Creativity and Innovation – DATA International Research Conference*, Wellesbourne: DATA. Online. Available at: http://www.bathspa.ac.uk/schools/education/projects/creative-teachers/default.asp (accessed 20 December 2010).

Department for Education and Skills (DfES) (2003) *Excellence and Enjoyment*, London: DfES.

Department for Education and Skills (2006) *Government Response to Paul Roberts' Report on Nurturing Creativity in Young People*, London: Department for Culture, Media and Sport.

Diakidoy, I-A.N. and Kanari, E. (1999) 'Student teachers' beliefs about creativity', *British Educational Research Journal*, 25(2): 225–43.

Dickinson, V.L., Abd-El-Khalick, F.S. and Lederman, N.G. (2000) *Changing Elementary Teachers' Views of the NOS: Effective Strategies for Science Method Courses*, ERIC Report no. ED 441 680.

Edmonds, J. (2004) 'Creativity in science; leaping the void', in R. Fisher and M. Williams (eds) *Unlocking Creativity*, London: David Fulton.

Esquivel, G.R.(1995) 'Teacher behaviours that foster creativity', *Educational Psychology Review*, 7: 185–202.

Euster, J.R. (1987) 'Fostering creativity and innovation', *College Research Library*, 48: 287–8.

Fernstermacher, G.D. and Soltis, J.F. (1986) *Approaches to Teaching*, New York: Teachers College Press.

Fisher, R. (1990) *Teaching Children to Think*, Hemel Hempstead: Simon and Schuster.

Fryer, M. and Collings, J.A. (1991) 'Teachers' views about creativity', *British Journal of Educational Psychology*, 61: 207–19.

Gardner, H. (1993) *Creating Minds*, New York: Basic Books.

Garner, R. (2007) 'Schools "must do more for creativity"', *The Independent*, 31 October 2007, p. 7.

Glück, J., Ernst, R. and Unger, F. (2002) 'How creatives define creativity: definitions reflect different types of creativity', *Creativity Research Journal*, 14(1): 55–67.

Gouge, K. and Yates, C. (2002) 'Creating a CA programme in the arts: the Wigan LEA arts project', in M. Shayer and P. Adey (eds) *Learning and Intelligence: cognitive acceleration across the curriculum from 5 to 15 years*, Buckingham: Open University.

Grainger, T and Barnes, J. (2006) 'Creativity in the primary curriculum', in J. Arthur, T. Grainger and D. Wray (eds) *Learning to Teach in the Primary School*, London: Routledge, pp. 209–25.

Harrington, D.M. (1990) 'The ecology of human creativity', in M.A. Runco and R.S. Albert (eds) *Theories of Creativity*, London: Sage.

Harvey, J. (1999) *Music and Inspiration*, London: Faber and Faber.

Haydon, L. (2008) *Engaging Primary School Learners through a Creative Curriculum*, Online. Available at: www.standards.dfes.gov.uk/ntrp (accessed 2 November 2010).

Howe, A. (2004) 'Science is creative', *Primary Science Review*, 81: 14–16.

Illich, I. (1971) *De-schooling Society*, London: Calder and Boyars.

Kennedy, M. (2005) *Inside Teaching: How Classroom Life Undermines Reform*, Cambridge, MA: Harvard University Press.

Kwang, N.A. (2001) *Why Asians are Less Creative than Westerners*, Singapore: Prentice-Hall.

MacWhinney, B. (2005) 'Language evolution and human development', in D. Bjorklund and A. Pellegrini (eds) *Origins of the Social Mind*, New York: Guilford.

Maker, C.J., Sonmi, J. and Muammar, O.M. (2008) 'Development of creativity', *Learning and Individual Differences*, 18: 402–17.

Massey, A. and Burnard, S. (2006) 'Here's one I made earlier!' *Emotional and Behavioural Difficulties*, 11(2): 121–33.

McLaren, R.B. (1999) 'Dark side of creativity', in M.A. Runco and S.R. Pritzker (eds.) *Encyclopedia of Creativity*, San Diego: Academic Press.

Merleau-Ponty, M. (1964) *Signs*, Evanston: North-western University Press.

Miller, G. (2000) *The Mating Mind: how sexual choice shaped the evolution of human nature*, London: Heinemann.

Mithen, S. (1996) *The Prehistory of the Mind*, London: Thames and Hudson.

Moseley, D., Baumfield, V., Elliott, J., Gregson, M., Higgins, S. Miller, J. and Newton, D.P. (2005) *Frameworks for Thinking*, Cambridge: Cambridge University Press.

Newton, D.P. (2011) *Teaching for Understanding*, London: Routledge.

Newton, D.P. and Newton, L.D. (2006) 'Could elementary textbooks serve as models of practice to help new teachers and non-specialists attend to reasoning in music?' *Music Education Research*, 8(1): 3–16.

Newton, L.D. and Newton, D.P. (2010) 'Creative thinking and teaching for creativity in elementary school science', *Gifted and Talented International*, 25(3): 111–23.

National Advisory Committee on Creative and Cultural Education (NACCCE) (1999) *All Our Futures: creativity, culture and education*, London: Department for Education and Employment.

Office for Standards in Education (Ofsted) (2006) *Creative Partnerships: initiative and impact*, Ref. no. HMI 2517, London: Ofsted.

Osborne, T. (2003) 'Against "creativity": a philistine rant', *Economy and Society*, 32(4): 507–25.

Park, S., Soo-Young, L., Oliver, S. and Cramond, B. (2006) 'Changes in Korean science teachers' perceptions of creativity and science teaching after participating in an overseas professional development program', *Journal of Science Teacher Education*, 17(1): 37–64.

Pehkonen, E. (1997) 'The state-of-art in mathematical creativity', *International Journal on Mathematical Education*, 29(3): 63–7.

Petty, G. (1997) *How to be Better at Creativity*, London: Kogan Page.

Piaget, J. (1932) *The Moral Judgment of the Child*, London: Routledge.

Prentice, R. (2000) 'Creativity: a reaffirmation of its place in early childhood education', *Curriculum Journal*, 11(2): 145–58.

Qualifications and Curriculum Authority (QCA) (2005) *Creativity: find it, promote it!* London: QCA.

Richards, R. (1993) 'Everyday creativity, eminent creativity and psychopathology', *Psychological Inquiry*, 4(3): 212–17.

Ritchie, S.M. and Edwards, J. (1996) 'Creative thinking instruction for aboriginal children', *Learning and Instruction*, 6(1): 59–75.

Runco, M.A. and Johnson, D.J. (2002) 'Parents' and teachers' implicit theories of children's creativity: a cross cultural perspective', *Creativity Research Journal*, 14: 427–38.

Schwartz-Geschka, M. (1994) 'Creativity in Japanese society', *Creativity and Innovation Management*, 3(4): 229–32.

Scottish Executive Education Department (SEED) (2006) *Promoting Creativity in Education: overview of key national policy developments across the UK*. Online. Available at: http://www.hmie.gov.uk/documents/publications/hmiepcie.html (accessed 14 December 2010).

Seefeldt, C. (1995) 'Art – a serious work', *Young Children*, 50: 39–42.

Shallcross, D.J. (1981) *Creative Thinking*, Englewood Cliffs, NJ: Prentice Hall.

Sternberg, R.J. (2006) 'The nature of creativity', *Creativity Research Journal*, 18(1): 87–98.

Tan, A-G. (2000) 'A review of the study of creativity in Singapore', *Journal of Creative Behavior*, 34(4): 259–84.

Tatarkiewicz, W. (1980) *A History of Six Ideas: an essay in aesthetics*, The Hague: Martinus Nijhoff.

Taylor, R. (1999) 'The meaning of life', *Philosophy Now*, 24: 8–10.

Thurstone, L. (1952) 'Creative talent', in L. Thurstone (ed.) *Applications of Psychology*, New York: Hillsdale.

Torrance, E.P. (1975) 'Explorations in creative thinking in the early school years', in C.W. Taylor and F. Barron (eds) *Scientific creativity: its recognition and development*, New York: Krieger.

Treffinger, D.J., Young, G.C., Selby, E.C. and Shepardson, C. (2002) *Assessing Creativity: a guide for educators*, Storrs: The National Research Centre on the Gifted and Talented.

Waters-Adams, S. (2006) 'The relationship between understanding the nature of science and practice: the influence of teachers' beliefs about education, teaching and learning', *International Journal of Science Education*, 28(8): 919–44.

Wegerif, R. (2010) *Mind Expanding*, Maidenhead: Open University Press.

Williams, F.E. (1970) *Classroom Ideas for Encouraging Thinking and Feeling*, Buffalo: DOK Publishers.

Wolpert, L. (2003) 'Understanding procrastination from a self-regulated learning perspective', *Journal of Educational Psychology*, 95(1): 179–87.

Creativity in English

Lynn Newton and David Waugh

Introduction

During a recent visit to a doctor's surgery, one of the authors observed the following.

> A small child, about 4 years old, was waiting with his older sister (about 7 years) and their father. The latter was checking his messages on his mobile 'phone and texting replies. The child was watching carefully and suddenly asked:
>
> BOY: Can I have your phone?
> FATHER: Why?
> BOY: [Pause] 'Cos I want to text somebody.
> FATHER: You can have it if you can spell 'text'.
>
> After a longer pause, during which the boy was clearly thinking hard, he went to the children's corner where his sister was playing. He quietly asked her to spell 'text' for him. His sister whispered, 't – e – x – t'.
>   The child returned to his father and resumed the conversation.
>
> BOY: 't – e – [long pause] a – b – c – d – ....'
>
> He never did get to 'x' as they were called in to the doctor's office.

This little boy clearly showed evidence of creativity and problem solving in the context of language use.

In a detailed review of the many definitions of creativity in various documents, Compton (2007) identified six key skills underpinning creative thinking as enquiry, evaluation, ideation, imagination, innovation and problem solving. These are skills accessible to most people, thus reinforcing that notion that everyone can be creative to some degree (Boden 2004; Torrance 1975). Such skills are used in activities that result in outcomes judged to be of worth and novelty, at least to the person creating them [National Advisory Committee on Creative and Cultural Education (NACCCE) 1999]. Even if an outcome has already been 'discovered', Thurstone (1952) argued that, if it is new to the individual (the child), then it is a creative act. Since children lack the experiences and knowledge of adults, they can have novel ideas and produce creative products that are new to them if not to the adults around them. An increase in achievement and improvement in motivation, self-esteem, social skills and behaviour have all been noted in situations where creative thinking has been encouraged [Qualifications and Curriculum Authority (QCA) 2003, 2005; Office for Standards in Education (Ofsted) 2006]. This in itself would seem to justify teaching *for* creativity in any subject. Yet, despite teachers being urged to foster creativity and problem-solving skills [Department for Education and Skills (DfES) 2003; Burke Hensley 2004; Hall and Thomson 2005) there is evidence that schools tend to ignore it (Garner 2007).

Part of the problem is that, like understanding, creativity is polymorphic in nature – its attributes vary from subject to subject (Newton 2012). Primary teachers might know what constitutes creativity in general but they also need to know what constitutes creative thought in the context of the individual subjects like elementary school English in order to foster it in a systematic way. Also, being creative is something that our pupils must do for themselves. Teachers can encourage them and scaffold the process by providing opportunities for creative thought (Weisberg 1988; Nickerson 1999; Newton 2012). However, ultimately, pupils must be able to be creative even when the teacher is not there.

Language and creativity in the primary classroom

Language is unique to humans. It enables us to construct representations of ideas and events. Further, we can use our language to control those ideas and events and over time this can have consequences, for both individuals and societies. So once language – any language – is available to a child, mental representation is possible, leading to mental model construction and deeper, alternative forms of thinking and learning.

In an international comparison of English as a second or additional language in the UK, Hungary and Switzerland, Spiro (2007) found that, at all levels, from primary aged pupils through to adults (teachers and undergraduate students), we hold similar views of what counts as creativity. Creativity as a process (a way of thinking and working) is what Grainger (2005: 197, cited in Spiro 2007: 79) calls 'a kind of passionate and playful intensity'. Theirs is a view that sees creative processing in language as both chaotic and ordered. Inspirational thinking at the individual level is, by its very nature, chaotic. However, it is ordered because the end-products, the creative outcomes, are shaped and moulded in line with social, cultural aesthetic rules and constraints. Spiro argues that, 'Writing creatively is not limited to the chosen and talented few, but an aspect of every language user's skill …' (Spiro 2007: 79). There is no reason to believe that these views would not also apply in the context of other languages and therefore have consequences for the teaching of those other languages.

In her book on language arts teaching in the USA, Lundsteen (1989) identifies clearly the two main challenges facing teachers. First, because language use is fundamental to all areas of the curriculum, there is a need for a broad range of language skills. Second, children are different in what they bring to the classroom in terms of experience and expertise in language. In her book, she focuses on English language arts, although the principles she puts forward apply to most languages.

In the UK, 'language' as a subject in the school curriculum is usually described as English (as opposed to the teaching of other languages, ancient or modern) and is a core area of the National Curriculum [Department for Education and Employment (DfEE)/ QCA 1999] and the specific strategies that underpin effective communication as literacy. English as a subject encompasses the four components of reading, writing, speaking and listening, which in turn incorporate elements like composition, spelling, punctuation, literature, debate, drama and poetry. In addition, over the last two decades in the UK, there has been push to raise standards in the language skills through a government-initiated National Literacy Strategy, replaced in 2003 by the Primary National Strategy, *Excellence and Enjoyment* (DfES 2003). The focus in such initiatives has been on raising standards in reading, with writing, speaking and listening receiving much less political attention. Yet we would argue that it is these very areas – composition of stories and poetry, critique of literature, debate, drama and so on – that lend themselves to productive opportunities for creative thought. In addition, there is a complex interaction between all of these different areas.

Lundsteen (1989) expands the language arts curriculum in the USA to include oral and written composition in other subject areas, investigation of linguistic systems, and responses to literature in all subject areas. She also emphasizes the interdependency and complex interaction between these areas and elements. Interestingly, the requirements of the other subjects of the National Curriculum in England and Wales show only a very low level of engagement with language development.

In a discussion of policy documents for language and literacy in the UK, Hall (2001) reviewed both the National Curriculum for English and the National Literacy Strategy. She considered the Literacy Strategy was the government's perceived solution to the problems of a decline in literacy standards and teacher incompetence at delivering the National Curriculum. Woods (2001), also discussing the National Literacy Strategy, argued that skills to develop creativity were being lost in the drive to teach grammar, punctuation and parts of speech. At the more general level of literacy skills, Hilton (2006) criticizes the use of Key Stage (KS) 2 (age 11) tests in England as a measure of literacy attainment and comments on the damaging consequences for creativity. Similarly there have been studies of language development through creative arts projects, highlighting the positive consequences for creative thought of removing National Curriculum and Literacy Strategy constraints. For example, Safford and Barrs (2007) carried out two studies of children's language and literacy development in the context of their work in a school-based creative arts project.

Although creativity in both its nature and outcomes has been well researched, what counts as creativity in different disciplines has been less well studied. In English (as a subject area in the curriculum at the primary or elementary school level), there have been a number of studies of creativity in different aspects of the subject and are summarized in Table 2.1.

TABLE 2.1 Studies of creative activity in different aspects of English

ASPECT OF ENGLISH	RESEARCHER(S)	FOCUS
Reading	Giorgis and Johnson (2001)	The inherent creativity of children's literature
	Pahl (2007)	Multimodal texts and the use of different question types to encourage creativity
Writing	Myhill (2001)	Importance of the writer's 'voice' in writing, crafting and creativity, and writing for meaning
	Whitely (2002)	The relationship between literacy and creativity through an exploration of children's writing and the genre of fables
	Fisher (2006)	Control in the teaching of writing
	Fraser (2006)	The creative potential of metaphorical writing in elementary schools
	Wilson, Jones and Wyse (2007)	Literary forms, creativity and teaching poetry writing
	Rojas-Drummond, Albarran and Littleton (2008)	Co-construction of oral and written texts through collaborative activity
	Cremin (2010)	Teachers as writers and teaching for creativity in writing
Speaking and listening	Vass (2002, 2007)	Exploration of the nature of paired talk and the role of friendship and peer pairing in collaborative creative writing tasks
	Wegerif (2005)	Verbal creativity versus explicit verbal reasoning and exploratory talk (explored as part of a study of reason, creativity and classroom dialogue)
	Rojas-Drummond *et al.* (2006)	Project exploring reasoning and productive talk. (Although this was with slightly older pupils, 11–12 years, the results are still relevant.)

While these studies have focused on creativity within aspects of the subject of English, there has been much less work on conceptions of creativity in English. In a study of primary pupils' perspectives of creative learning, Jeffrey (2001) identified the facets of pupils' engagement that assists creative learning. He advised teachers to encourage pupils to:

■ explain innovative procedures;

■ produce unique objects/solutions/presentations;

- experiment;
- ask questions concerning either facts/knowledge or process;
- summarize their experiences;
- use metaphor; and
- make contributions to the curriculum or pedagogic approach or problem.

Teachers' conceptions of creativity in English

Research shows that teachers' views of creativity worldwide are similar and relatively stable over time, at least at the general level (Bjerstedt 1976; Fryer and Collings 1991; Diakidoy and Kanari 1999; Runco and Johnson 2002). Creativity is seen as involving original, independent work, practised largely in the arts subjects. It was also noted that some subjects were seen as offering fewer opportunities for creative thought than others. But teachers' conceptions are complex (Hardy and Kirkwood 1994) and influenced by factors such as the nature of a subject itself, lack of personal subject knowledge, limited teaching experience, preferred teaching and learning approaches, and pressure to deliver specific content (Fryer and Collings 1991; Brickhouse and Bodner 1992).

Research has been carried out on teachers' conceptions of creativity in subject areas like mathematics (Bolden, Harries and Newton 2010), science (Newton and Newton, 2009, 2010) and history (Blake *et al.* 2010). However, there is limited evidence of teachers' conceptions of creativity within the subject area of English. A recent study by Newton and Beverton (2012, in press) identified notions of creativity in primary school English held by teachers in training to determine how appropriate they were for teaching English as an primary school curriculum subject. The group were not specialists in English and none had had any formal instruction on creativity or teaching for creativity, yet they would all eventually teach in UK primary schools (5–11-year-olds) across the full curriculum, including English.

Taken together, the trainees appear to conform to the general views of creativity as favouring the arts. While most saw English as a creative subject, all saw art and drama as more creative than English and mathematics as less creative. Other subjects were more randomly distributed, although subjects like music, and design and technology tended to be seen as offering more opportunities for creative thought than English.

The trainees were also asked to comment upon their views of English lessons they had seen or taught and opportunities for creativity they provided. The most frequent responses were to do with lessons involving story and poetry writing and literature activities (such as fairy tales). When asked about the creative elements of these lessons they identified them as lessons in which children use their own ideas, imagery and imagination; choose their own topics; and have no limits or constraints on them, with freedom to explore. The trainees identified areas like dramatic performances, poetry writing, giving verbal explanations and group discussion as providing the greatest opportunities for creativity. On the other hand, aspects such as reading non-fiction, handwriting and presentation work, and listening to factual descriptions were considered to offer the least opportunity for creative thought.

When the trainees responses were sorted, their notions produced three distinct clusters. There was a major *cognitive* cluster (62 per cent) to do with the development of productive thought (e.g. through use of children's imagination, their own ideas, problem solving, critical thinking, etc.). There were also two minor clusters. One (25 per cent) was to do with the *locus of control*, the teacher or the learner (e.g. degree of freedom, decisions as to what will be done and why, removal of curricular barriers or assessment constraints, etc.). The other (13 per cent) was to do with *behaviour* and with *physical activity* or *interaction* (e.g. opportunity for paired work, discussion, movement, interaction through role play, etc.).

The majority of the trainees expressed the view that encouraging creative thought in English was easy to do. Some said it depended upon *either* the child *or* the lesson/topic being taught. One person said it depended on whether it was a girl or a boy, boys being harder to motivate to think creatively. Few students provided an open comment although one said 'it takes a creatively thinking teacher to be creative with the English curriculum', reflecting the common confusion between teaching creatively and teaching for creativity. So how can we encourage primary teachers to be teachers who promote creative thinking in English?

According to Nystrand and Zeiser (1970), pupils vary in creative capability, depending upon a number of factors: the nature of the task itself; the learners' own level of independence; and their willingness to depart from the norm. Russ (1996), in her exploration of the development of creative processes in children, looked at three sets of process: cognitive (e.g. divergent and transformational thinking); affective (e.g. openness and pleasure in challenge and problem solving); and personality (e.g. curiosity, tolerance of ambiguity and willingness to take risks). She argued that all three are important but it is the way the sets interact with each other that generates the different creative profiles of individuals and hence different creative outcomes. However, it cannot be assumed that opportunities for creative thinking will always be well received. Torrance (1975) found that some children can react negatively to others being creative, resulting in peer pressure adversely affecting creative behaviour. So in an inclusive classroom, where every child is being encouraged to achieve his or her creative potential, teachers need to know how to support creative thought.

Teaching for creative thought in English and other languages

A number of studies have explored the kinds of activity used in lessons to encourage creative thought and problem solving in language lessons. In this last section, we explore some of these that have particular relevance to developing creative thought with primary school children and then suggest some ideas as starting points for teachers to use in language classrooms.

Play

In the UK, the Plowden Report [Central Advisory Council for Education (England) (CACE), 1967] argued that inventiveness and imagination – both aspects of creativity – could be developed and nurtured through play. In her exploration of how sets of processes inter- act when children are being creative, Russ (1996) focused particularly on affective pro- cesses and play. She suggested that, for creativity, the most important type of play is pretend play, with its fantasy and symbolism. Scully and Roberts (2002), in a study of the impor- tance of play in the instruction of reading and writing, found that children whose early literacy experiences included pleasurable activities were more likely to be motivated to learn and pursue more challenging, authentic tasks. They suggest teachers think about stimulating children's imagination (an aspect of creativity) through play.

Spiro (2007) proposes a range of activities to help to develop learners' creative thinking through playing with language. For example, she suggests the following.

- *Word sorts* – lists of words to sort into positive and negative groups; compare and explain why (e.g. crow/bird; 13/3; witch/wizard; …).

- *Choose and write about one word* (number or colour) and what it means for them (e.g. 13 = unlucky; red = danger).

- *Word similes* – explain and expand the associations (e.g. school is like a …; homework is like a …; my brother/sister is like a …).

- *I remember game* – focus on a vivid memory from the past and use all five senses to describe it, first orally then in writing (e.g. use objects, places, people, events, colours, sounds, smells.

- *Visualize game* – using imagination to create the unknown (e.g. What is in the box? Who is behind the door? What is the noise? Then, lift the lid, open the door, find the source of the noise).

Active learning and problem solving

An abandonment of prescribed curricula in favour of curricula that encourage enquiry- based or discovery-based learning is proposed by Burke Hensley (2004). This very much reflects that broader set of thinking skills that underpins the problem-solving strategies mentioned earlier and ties in to Scully and Roberts (2002) authentic experiences and challenges considered earlier. Burke Hensley (2004: 32) argues that such active curricula value creativity and encourage a 'creative and questioning environment'. In such an envi- ronment he argues that curiosity and creativity go hand in hand because the learners can suspend previous knowledge and beliefs, cross boundaries, take risks and take ownership of their own learning.

In a longitudinal study of a small group of KS2 children (7–11 years) with poor lan- guage development in a UK special school for children with social, emotional and behav- ioural difficulties, Massey and Burnard (2006) explored the use of project-based learning with the pupils. They set up a weekly project hour where the pupils could choose from four activities: designing a model; drawing or painting; making a photograph book; or making a book. Over the academic year they looked for evidence of independent and imaginative learning. While there was adult support for the children, the latter were devel- oping and using their own ideas. Massey and Burnard found these projects increased pupils' motivation and improved their problem solving and thinking skills.

Writing craft

Young learners are required to write a remarkable amount each school day but the process of writing is often simply the medium through which other learning activities are judged. Myhill (2001) expresses concern about this and about standards in writing. She argues that, although teachers are often giving children ownership of the writing experience, this does not equate to creativity or to the freedom to use a personal voice. She notes that studies of writing, both in English (the subject) and across the curriculum, indicate that teachers tend to define the writing tasks (what to write about) rather than teach about the generation of ideas and the means of expression in writing (how to do it). She suggests a need to re-conceptualize the teaching of writing to acknowledge not only the significance of the writer's voice but also the teaching about how written texts create meaning. She describes this as the dual activity of creating and crafting.

The involvement of professional experts – artists, writers, poets or dramatists – has already been mentioned. Spiro (2007), exploring the teaching of poetry, considers the involvement of a poet in residence. Her focus was on the use of an expert as an authentic strategy to promote creative thought and expository writing. She obtained positive responses from the pupils, with enhanced learning and motivation. While no age range is specified, it seems an effective strategy for primary learners. She discusses a range of writing strategies that can be used with learners of any age to promote creative thinking.

Drama and performance arts

This is an area in which there have been a number of studies in the past two decades. In her 1998 study, Cremin focused on creativity in English and drama. She discussed three components: the sources of imagination; the context of improvisation; and originality as a criterion of quality. A meta-analysis of studies of creativity, drama and verbal skills was carried out by Podlozny (2000) who found positive effects of drama as a tool for increasing achievement in story understanding, reading and writing. However, weak results were obtained for vocabulary development. They also noted variability according to types of drama.

Work by O'Day (2001) integrated creative drama and language arts to help children build their literacy skills. She looked at supporting language development through teacher-scaffolded plays with a first grade reading class. Having noticed a lack of appropriate material to fit the needs of young children, she wrote her own play, including non-speaking parts. The children had to use their imaginations to fill in blanks, think about what something or someone would be like or how someone would respond to a situation. The children were encouraged to bring their own interests, experiences and interpretations to the story line. Eventually, the children began to create their own story lines, short plays and then longer plays. Through this they also began to take their thinking across the curriculum, particularly into history. They explored the life of real writers of plays and the historical contexts in which they worked.

In the UK, Prendeville (2000) provided some information on drama in the National Curriculum for English. He was particularly interested in the teachers when 'in role' and put forward the idea of drama as a story game, with the teacher as one of the members of the story. Through the process, all participants had to learn the rules of the game and Prendeville provides several examples of this in the classroom.

Using music and the arts

Studies where the focus has been on the development of oral language and literacy learning through the integration of visual performance arts, literature, music and crafts have included an elementary school project in the US entitled *Art-full Reading and Writing* (Grant *et al.* 2008). Their work was aimed at improving performance on state literacy tests by combining the arts with language learning. Similarly, in the UK, Brice Heath and Wolf (2005) worked with KS1 pupils (aged 4–7 years) on a Creative Partnership project to explore art and language development. The school hosted an artist in residence who introduced visual arts (drawing and painting) alongside language (the associated talk to do with 3 and 4 syllable technical terms, biographies of artists, and critiques of artists' works). The researchers showed an increase in the children's manual and linguistic work requiring attention to detail, their understanding of and receptivity to complex terms and processes, and their familiarity with the analytical and sequential thinking needed to solve problems.

Using multimedia

In recent years, the use of multimedia to support learning has grown enormously. For example, Loveless (2003), thinking about information and communications technology (ICT) in the UK, produced a framework describing creativity as an interaction between people, processes, domains and the wider social and cultural context, and related these to definitions of ICT capability in the National Curriculum. ICT as a tool to extend capabilities was used by Halloran *et al.* (2006) on a field trip used to support literacy learning with a class of 9–10-year-olds. The context for this was historical but such ICT tools can be used in other areas of the curriculum (e.g. in science with the use of sensors to gather ecological data). In a study of 10-year-olds in Australia, Vincent (2007) discusses their struggle with verbal text. He used a multimedia approach to link ICT and literacy skills and to encourage 'envisioning' writing, generating positive outcomes.

In the context of promoting creativity in the classroom, Watts (2007) used film as a creative, engaging and effective strategy for teaching reading. This approach used moving image as an alternative text to printed books. In the small-scale research project the children made their own films, taking on the roles of director, film crew, sound technicians, illustrators and narrators. Watts argued that the effectiveness was a result of the children thinking for themselves. Their discussions came naturally, there was sense of excitement, motivation and engagement with the learning and change in the learner–teacher relationship. Similarly, Harrett and Benjamin (2009) used television media experiences (the BBC television science fiction series *Dr Who*) to enhance literacy with 8–11-year-old pupils and raise writing standards. In their paper 'Travel with a time lord', they describe how a group of ten primary teachers in Wales were made more aware of the potential of media resources to enhance learning and creativity.

Some further suggestions for language activities that encourage creative thinking and problem solving on the part of the young learners are given in Tables 2.2–2.6.

TABLE 2.2 Ideas for language: creative starters

FOCUS	ACTIVITIES
Playing with words and sounds	– Word building; word hunts; word games; word rhythms (e.g. Dr Seuss's *Cat in the Hat*)
Reading aloud	– Stories or rhymes for listening: read by a teacher, other adult or an older child (e.g. traditional rhymes and tales; popular contemporary stories)
	– Stories or rhymes that encourage active participation (e.g. Simon says; Chinese whispers)
	– Stories or rhymes that encourage follow-up experience
Ideas, expository writing	– Pictures and paintings (e.g. in Breughel's picture of the harvest collection, what are the people talking about?)
	– An event (e.g. following a field trip to a working water mill, write about a day in the miller's life, create a new bread recipe, etc.)
	– Starters: concrete objects, children choose for themselves which to focus on (e.g. small mechanical and wind-up toys in design technology; plastic bugs and insects in science, historical TV characters, etc.)
	– Starters: common objects (e.g. a training shoe tells its story; a day in the life of a pound coin; etc.)
	– Starters: unusual objects (teacher suggested) (e.g. imagine who owned this Roman coin; describe the journey of a piece of meteorite; life in an abandoned paper wasps nest; etc.)
	– Endings: tell part of a familiar story or rhyme and ask children change the ending (e.g. what might have happened if Cinderella hadn't heard the clock strike midnight?)

TABLE 2.3 Ideas for creative activities in English teaching in the primary school: nursery/reception

LANGUAGE FOCUS	CREATIVE ACTIVITY
Play/games	Games that relate words to actions help young children to develop their vocabularies. In PE and movement, ask them to move in different ways (*quickly, slowly, sadly, happily*) and use a variety of verbs to match to their actions (*run, jump, leap, hop,* etc.).
Reading: phonics/word level	Children need to develop their ability to discriminate between sounds. Make a simple sound box and show the children different objects which can make a noise (e.g. a bell, a rattle, a box of sweets). Put the objects in the box so that children can't see them, then rattle, shake, etc. and ask children to identify the source of the sounds. Add more items as the children progress and let them take turns to make the noises.
Reading: text level	Sharing stories is an essential part of language and literacy development at this stage. Use picture books as well as those with text. Make story sacks with artefacts related to the stories, such as a basket and a cloak for *Red Riding Hood*. Ask children to join in with repetitive dialogue (e.g. 'Oh Grandma, what big …').
Writing: stories and rhymes	Write stories with children through shared writing, drawing upon their ideas and modelling the writing process. Read and recite simple poems and songs and ask children to think of alternative rhyming words. They should do this orally, but you could write them down so that they can see how sounds relate to letters.
Writing: for a purpose	Children's writing may be very limited at this stage, but they can make use of their emergent writing to make lists (e.g. taking orders in a class 'restaurant'). Their writing may not be easily related to the English lexicon, but it is likely that some will include letters and even words.
Speaking discussion	Young children need lots of opportunities to talk with adults and with other children. Pose questions (e.g. *why do you think it is usually colder at night than during the daytime?*) and ask them to discuss in pairs and then share their ideas with a larger group.
Speaking: drama	The 'home corner' is an important stimulus for dramatic activity. Change the nature of the corner from time to time or create other areas for structured play, such as a shop, doctor's surgery, pizza restaurant or kitchen. Encourage children to take on the roles of different people and to talk in role.
Listening	When reading poems to children, try pausing at a rhyming word and ask them to suggest one. Play *opposites* with them, giving them words and asking them to say an opposite, e.g. hot–cold, high–low, large–small. This can be extended to sentences (e.g. 'He liked his new bike' – 'He didn't like his new bike').

TABLE 2.4 Ideas for creative activities in English teaching in the primary school: Y1—2

LANGUAGE FOCUS	CREATIVE ACTIVITY
Play/games	Ask children to work in pairs in PE and movement, with each taking a turn to close eyes or be blindfolded while the other guides them using oral directions. Get children to demonstrate for the rest of the class, and talk about the kind of words that are useful – *turn*, *stop*, *left*, *right*, etc.
Reading: phonics/ word level	Children should now be familiar with many letter-sound correspondences, but still need to develop their ability to discriminate between sounds. Play odd one out games, using words at an appropriate level and asking them to pick which, for example, has a different ending/beginning/middle sound (e.g. *bad, lap, lad; bash, bud, car; hot, bat, lot*).
Reading: text level	Shared reading, in which extracts from texts are displayed so that children can follow your reading and then read with you, helps develop their understanding of reading techniques. Make them more aware of punctuation by asking them to pause at commas and full stops. Make word cards and punctuation cards and invite children to the front of the class to hold them up, while the rest of the class suggest ways in which they might be arranged to make sentences. Give one child a question mark and ask children to suggest ways in which some sentences might be changed into questions.
Writing: stories and rhymes	Use traditional tales as a starting point for children's story-telling and story-writing. For example, they might listen to and discuss or re-enact *The Three Little Pigs* and then produce their own story on similar lines but perhaps with different characters and/or setting.
Writing: for a purpose	As children develop their writing skills, encourage them to write for each other (e.g. on paper or mini-whiteboards they could write notes and messages to each other). They can also make notices and labels and signs for their classroom. At the end of Y2, children could produce guides to their classroom for the next Y2 class.
Speaking: discussion	Give children plenty of opportunities to discuss ideas and to plan and work together. Encourage them to *think-pair-share* when you ask questions, so that they think about an answer, share it with a partner and then one of the pair provides an answer.
Speaking: drama	Children can engage in role play related to stories and poems at this stage. After reading a story to them, get children to 'hot-seat' and be asked questions by others, which they must answer in role as a character from the story.
Listening	Read and discuss part of a non-fiction text and then read it again, but include some mistakes for children to spot. These might be factual errors or they could be grammatical.

TABLE 2.5 Ideas for creative activities in English teaching in the primary school: Y3—4

LANGUAGE FOCUS	CREATIVE ACTIVITY
Play/games	Play language games such as *I spy* to reinforce letter-sound correspondences and spelling. Give children cards with individual graphemes as a starting point for games and challenges (e.g. 'Can you make a word with four phonemes?' 'What is the longest word you can make? How many words can you make which begin with a consonant digraph?')
Reading: phonics/word level	Children should now be familiar with all common phoneme–grapheme correspondences, but games and other activities can help reinforce this knowledge. Ask them to produce alliterative sentences and poems to reinforce initial sounds. They can also look at a range of *tongue twisters* and then write their own.
Reading: text level	Encourage prediction by asking children to discuss and jot down their predictions for the next events in stories, when you pause when reading to them. Ask them to write the next paragraph, working in pairs to share ideas.
Writing: stories and rhymes	Ask children to make collections of rhyming words and encourage them to test their spellings and whether their words exist by looking in a dictionary (paper or online). Relate their findings to phoneme–grapheme correspondences and talk about different ways in which the same sounds can be written.
Writing: for a purpose	Letter-writing can be purposeful and result in responses. Ask children to write to: parents informing them about class assemblies, etc; curators at museums or galleries they might visit, asking for information; people who have visited the class, thanking them and asking questions; each other, but in role, perhaps as characters from a story they have been reading or listening to.
Speaking: discussion	Before visits or receiving visitors, ask children to discuss questions they might ask. These can later be written in letters (see earlier).
Speaking: drama	Provide scenarios for small-group drama, including those with the potential for argument and discussion, such as parents and children arguing about bedtime. Link drama to stories children read and hear, including asking small groups to act out their predicted next section of a story (see earlier).
Listening	Play *Chinese Whispers* by asking children to pass a message to a neighbour who then passes it on to another, etc. Ask the last person in the chain to tell the whole class the message, and then compare it with the original. Discuss the importance of clear messages and careful listening and re-telling.

TABLE 2.6 Ideas for creative activities in English teaching in the primary school: Y5—6

LANGUAGE FOCUS	CREATIVE ACTIVITY
Play/games	In PE and games, ask children to use a limited number of resources (e.g. a ball, two hoops and a post) to devise and try out games for others to play. They should then explain their games to other groups and show them how to play. Feedback from other groups can lead to modifications and finally written instructions so that children from other classes might play.
Reading: phonics/ word level	Explore morphemes with children and show how they can be used to modify words' meanings. Then play a morpheme game in which words with, say, three morphemes are hidden behind three flaps and children choose which part of the words they would like revealed (e.g. for *reported*, the three flaps would cover *re- port* and *-ed*). Once one morpheme has been revealed, children can see how many possible words might be revealed when the other flaps are lifted. For *reported*, if *re-* was the first morpheme revealed, they might think of *retired, reused, refusal*, etc.
Reading: text level	Make a collection of story openings from well-known books and display these together with copies of book covers. Ask children to read the openings and try to match them to the books. Ask them to make their own collections and use these as starting points for discussions on different ways in which readers' attentions can be *grabbed* so that they want to read on.
Writing: stories and rhymes	Introduce a poem such as *The Jabberwocky* by Lewis Carroll to children and ask them to discuss what the invented words might mean. Can they create their own nonsense words, drawing upon their knowledge of morphemes and write their own nonsense poems or an alternative version of *The Jabberwocky*?
Writing: for a purpose	Ask children to write story openings for others to continue. This might develop into group story writing, with stories being passed on from person to person or pair to pair to be continued.
Speaking: discussion	Using a plan or map and, perhaps, a model, create a town or village with the children. Ask them to talk about the facilities which would be needed and the people who might live there. Give children roles within the town and encourage them to talk to other characters in role. The town might be from an historical period they are studying and could lead to online research to find out more about how people lived.
Speaking: drama	Role play related to the town (see earlier) can involve children talking with members of the class with whom they might not normally have conversations. Devise scenarios for the townspeople to discuss, such as debates about new buildings, roads and bridges.
Listening	The BBC Radio 4 panel game *Just a Minute* in which panellists must talk about a given subject for 60 seconds without hesitating, deviating from the subject or repeating any words other than those in the subject, provides an interesting and challenging activity for Y5–6 children. Model the game yourself and ask children to say when you are guilty of hesitation, deviation or repetition. Then play the game with groups of children. (Editions of the radio programme can be found on the BBC iPlayer at http://www.bbc.co.uk/iplayer/)

References

Bjerstedt, A. (1976) *Explorations in creativity*, Lund: Liber Laromedel/Gleerup).

Blake, A., Edwards, G., Newton, D.P. and Newton, L.D. (2010) 'Some student teachers' conceptions of creativity in primary school history', *International Journal of Historical Learning, Teaching and Research*, 9(2): 15–23.

Boden, M.A. (2004) *The Creative Mind – Myths and Mechanisms*, London: Routledge.

Bolden, D., Harries, T. and Newton, D. (2010) 'Pre-service primary teachers' conceptions of creativity in mathematics', *Educational Studies in Mathematics*, 73: 143–57.

Brice Heath, S. and Wolf, S. (2005) 'Focus on creative learning: drawing on art for language development', *Literacy: The Journal of the United Kingdom Literacy Association*, Special Issue: Focus on Creative Learning, pp. 38–45.

Brickhouse, N. & Bodner, G.M. (1992) 'The beginning science teacher: classroom narratives of conviction and constraints', *Journal of Research in Science Teaching*, 29(5): 471–85.

Burke Hensley, R. (2004) 'Curiosity and creativity as attributes of information literacy', *Reference and User Services Quarterly*, 44(1): 31–6.

Central Advisory Council for Education (England) (CACE) (1967) *Children and their Primary Schools (The Plowden Report: Vol. 1)*, London: HMSO.

Compton, A. (2007) 'What does creativity mean in English education?' *Education 3–13*, 35(2): 109–16.

Cremin, M. (1998) 'The imagination, and originality, in English and classroom drama', *English in Education*, 32(2): 4–13.

Cremin, T. (2010) 'Creativity, uncertainty and discomfort: teachers as writers', *Cambridge Journal of Education*, 36(3): 415–33.

Department for Education and Employment/Qualifications and Curriculum Authority (DfEE/QCA) (1999) *National Curriculum for England: Science*, London: DfEE/QCA, p. 8.

Department for Education and Skills (DfES) (2003) *Excellence and Enjoyment*, London: DfES.

Diakidoy, I-A.N. and Kanari, E. (1999) 'Student teachers' beliefs about creativity', *British Educational Research Journal*, 25(2): 225–43.

Fisher, R. (2006) 'Whose writing is it anyway? Issues of control in the teaching of writing', *Cambridge Journal of Education*, 36(2): 193–206.

Fraser, D. (2006) 'The creative potential of metaphorical writing in the literacy classroom', *English Teaching: Practice and Critique*, 5(2): 93–108.

Fryer, M. & Collings, J.A. (1991) 'Teachers' views about creativity' *British Journal of Educational Psychology*, 61: 207–19.

Garner, R. (2007) 'Schools "must do more for creativity"', *The Independent*, 31 October 2007, p. 7.

Giorgis, C. and Johnson, N.J. (2001) 'Creativity', *The Reading Teacher*, 54(6): 632–40.

Grant, A., Hutchinson, K., Hornsby, D. and Brooke, S. (2005) 'Creative pedagogies: "Art-full" reading and writing', *English Teaching: Practice and Critique*, 7(1): 57–72.

Hall, C. and Thomson, P. (2005) 'Creative tensions? Creativity and basic skills in recent educational policy', *English in Education*, 39(3): 5–18.

Hall, K. (2001), 'An analysis of primary literacy policy in England using Barthes' notion of "readerly" and "writerly" texts', *Journal of Early Childhood Literacy*, 1(2): 153–65.

Halloran, J., Hornecker, E., Fitzpatrick, G., Weal, M., Millard, D., Michaelides, D., Cruickshank and De Roure, D. (2006) *The Literacy Fieldtrip: Using UbiComp to Support Children's Creative Writing*, ACM 1-59593-316-606007.

Hardy, T. & Kirkwood, V. (1994) 'Towards creating effective learning environments for science teachers', *International Journal of Science Education*, 16: 231–51.

Harrett, J. and Benjamin, T. (2009) 'Travels with a time lord: using media to enhance literacy', *Literacy: The Journal of the United Kingdom Literacy Association*, 43(3): 134–42.

Hilton, M. (2006) 'Damaging confusions in England's KS2 reading tests: a response to Anne Kispal', *Literacy*, 40(1): 36–41.

Jeffrey, B. (2001) 'Primary pupils' perspectives and creative learning', *Encyclopaideia 2001* [Italian], 5.9: 133–52.

Loveless, A. (2003) 'Creating spaces in the primary curriculum: ICT in creative subjects', *Curriculum Journal*, 14(1): 5–21.

Lundsteen, S.W. (1989) *Language Arts Teaching: A Problem-Solving Approach*, New York: Harper Row.

Massey, A. and Burnard, S. (2006) '"Here's one I made earlier!" A qualitative report on creativity in a residential primary school for children with social, emotional and behavioural difficulties', *Emotional and Behavioural Difficulties*, 11(2): 121–33.

Myhill, D. (2001) 'Writing: crafting and creating', *English in Education*, 35(3): 13–20.

National Advisory Committee on Creative and Cultural Education (1999) *All Our Futures: Creativity, Culture and Education*, London: DfEE.

Newton, D.P. (2012) *Teaching for Understanding: What it is and How to do it*, 2nd edn, London: Routledge.

Newton, D.P. and Newton, L.D. (2010) 'Some student teachers' conceptions of creativity in school science', *Research in Science and Technological Education*, 27(1): 45–60.

Newton, L. and Beverton, S. (2012, in press) 'Pre-service teachers' conceptions of creativity in elementary school English' *Thinking Skills and Creativity*.

Newton, L.D. and Newton, D.P. (2009) 'What teachers see as creative incidents in elementary science lessons', *International Journal of Science Education (Research Report)*, 32(15): 1989–2005.

Nickerson, R.S. (1999) 'Enhancing creativity', in R.J. Sternberg (ed.) *Handbook of Creativity*, Cambridge: Cambridge University Press, pp. 392–430.

Nystrand, M. and Zeiser, S. (1970) 'Dewey, Dixon, and the future of creativity', *The English Journal*, 59(8): 1138–40.

O'Day, S. (2001) 'Creative drama through scaffolded plays in the language arts classroom', *Primary Voices K-6*, 9(4): 20–5.

Office for Standards in Education (Ofsted) (2006) *Creative partnerships: initiative and impact* (Ref no. HMI 2517), London: Ofsted.

Pahl, K. (2007) 'Creativity in events and practices: a lens for understanding children's multimodal texts', *Literacy: The Journal of the United Kingdom Literacy Association*, 41(2): 86–92.

Podlozny, A. (2000) 'Strengthening verbal skills through the use of classroom drama: a clear link', *Journal of Aesthetic Education*, 34(3–4): 239–75.

Prendeville, F. (2000) 'Teacher in role' – The undercover agent in the classroom, *Education 3–13*, June: 9–14.

Qualifications and Curriculum Authority (QCA) (2003; 2005) *Creativity: Find It! Promote It!* London: QCA/DfEE.

Rojas-Drummond, S., Mazón, N. Fernández, M and Wegerif, R. (2006) 'Explicit reasoning, creativity and co-construction in primary school children's collaborative activities', *Thinking Skills and Creativity*, 1: 84–94.

Rojas-Drummond, S.M., Albarrán, C.D. and Littleton, K.S. (2008) 'Collaboration, creativity and the co-construction of oral and written texts', *Thinking Skills and Creativity*, 3: 177–91.

Runco, M.A. and Johnson, D.J. (2002) 'Parents' and teachers' implicit theories of children's creativity: a cross cultural perspective', *Creativity Research Journal*, 14: 427–38.

Russ, S.W. (1996) 'Development of creative processes in children', *New Directions in Child Development*, 72: 31–42.

Safford, K. and Barrs, M. (2007) 'Creating contexts for talk: the influence of a school-based creative arts project on children's language', *English in Education*, 41(2): 44–56.

Scully, P. and Roberts, H. (2002) 'Phonics, expository writing, and reading aloud: playful literacy in the primary grades', *Early Chidlhood Education Journal*, 30(2): 93–99.

Spiro, J. (2007) 'Teaching poetry: writing poetry – teaching as a writer', *English in Education*, 41(3): 78–93.

Thurstone, L. (1952, ed.) *Applications of Psychology*, New York: HarperCollins.

Torrance, E.P. (1975) 'Explorations in creative thinking in the early school years', in C.W. Taylor and F. Barron (eds) *Scientific creativity: its recognition and development*, New York: Krieger, pp. 173–83.

Vass, E. (2002) 'Friendship and collaborative creative writing in the primary classroom', *Journal of Computer Assisted Learning*, 18: 102–10.

Vass, E. (2007) 'Exploring processes of collaborative creativity – The role of emotions in children's joint creative writing', *Thinking Skills and Creativity*, 2: 107–17.

Vincent, J. (2007) 'Literacy, learning preferences and multimedia', *Journal of Artistic and Creative Education*, 1(1): 140–53.

Watts, R. (2007) 'Harnessing the power of film in the primary classroom', *Literacy: The Journal of the United Kingdom Literacy Association*, 41(2): 102–9.

Wegerif, R. (2005) 'Reason and creativity in classroom dialogues', *Language and Education*, 19(3): 223–37.

Weisberg, W. (1988) 'Problem solving and creativity', in: R.J. Sternberg (ed.) *The Nature of Creativity*, Cambridge, Cambridge University Press, pp. 148–76.

Whitely, D. (2002) 'Writing fables: genre and creativity', *English and Education*, 36(1): 16–24.

Wilson, A., Jones, K. and Wyse, D. (2007) 'Finding a voice? Do literary forms work creatively in teaching poetry writing?' *Cambridge Journal of Education*, 37(3): 441–57.

Woods, P. (2001) 'Creative Literacy', in Craft, A., Jeffrey, B. and Leibling, A. (eds) *Creativity in Education*, London: Continuum, pp. 62–79.

Creativity in Mathematics

David Bolden

Introduction

It is true that, historically, the act of being creative tends to be associated with the arts (see e.g. Douglas Newton's discussion in Chapter 1). As a result it is perhaps also true for many that the subject of mathematics, and particularly primary mathematics, may not be something that immediately comes to mind when one thinks about creativity. After all, isn't there always a right or wrong answer where mathematics is concerned? Isn't there little opportunity for freedom of expression in mathematics? This chapter aims to answer each of these questions with a resounding 'no' and argue for a very different view of primary mathematics, one in which creativity on the part of both the teacher and the pupil plays a central and important role.

Creativity in mathematics

It is important to say at the outset of this chapter that the concept of creativity is complex and beset by operational disagreement. Consequently, there is no universally agreed upon definition of creativity (Plucker *et al.* 2004) and thus no agreed upon definition of mathematical creativity (Sriraman 2009). Some emphasize the process, some the product and some both. Until relatively recently, creativity in mathematics was seen as the domain of only those extraordinary and gifted individuals who could produce new knowledge or a new way of doing things (Weisberg 1988; Sternberg 1988; Gruber and Wallace 2000). This has been termed 'the genius' or 'big C' view (Csikszentmihalyi 1996) of mathematical creativity. More recently, however, there has developed a more egalitarian notion of creativity. This notion views a creative act as one that is new to the self and therefore it allows for the possibility that everyone is capable of creative activity to some degree. This might be termed the 'little c' view of creativity but it also has other names (see e.g. Craft 2003). For instance, Boden (2004) agrees with this notion when she distinguishes between 'historical creativity', which describes an act that produces something novel to the world, and 'psychological creativity', which produces something new to the individual concerned. Others, too, accept that children sitting in mathematics classrooms are capable of creative thinking in mathematics (Sriraman 2005, 2008).

Consequently, this view of creativity is one that is relevant to the teaching of mathematics to young children.

Creativity in the primary mathematics classroom

The above reflects a shift from an absolutist view of creativity to a more relativistic view (Leikin, 2009). The former view is associated with the production of new ideas on a world stage, whereas the latter view allows for the possibility that school children can also show mathematical creativity. This latter view would see creativity in any number of simple classroom acts that we, as adults, would not necessarily view as particularly creative. For example, children are being creative in mathematics when they discover or derive a new number fact from an already known number fact, such as when a child spots and uses the proximity of $5 + 6$ to the known number fact of $5 + 5 = 10$ or when a child realizes that a number can be partitioned in many different ways other than just in the canonical form (e.g. that 12 can be partitioned canonically into $10 + 2$ but in other ways too: $8 + 4$ or $6 + 6$).

It is the act of problem solving that lies at the very heart of pupil creativity in the primary mathematics classroom (Silver 1997; Sriraman 2005). It was the Cockroft report in the UK (Cockroft 1982) that re-established problem solving as the heart of effective learning and teaching of mathematics, although many earlier researchers had never swayed from that belief. The Cockroft report was commissioned by the UK government at the time as a result of concerns that young children were not developing the necessary mathematical skills and understandings, especially in mental calculation, and that teachers were relying too heavily on published schemes in their teaching. The report argued that 'the ability to solve problems is at the heart of mathematics' (Cockcroft 1982: 249), and so it included in its list of recommendations that problem solving be better integrated into the primary mathematics curriculum.

This official recognition of problem solving as central to the effective learning and teaching of mathematics would have been warmly welcomed by those researchers who had long been advocates of using children's problem-solving ability as a measure of mathematical creativity (e.g. Guildford 1967; Torrance 1974). In particular, it was children's ability to show divergent thinking when presented with mathematical problems which was their criteria for creativity. Divergent thinking is often contrasted with convergent thinking, which is the process of identifying the one and only one solution to a given problem (so often the end-result of much mathematical problem-solving in schools). Divergent thinking is the process of identifying many solutions and so is often measured in terms of children's ability to show *flexibility*, *fluency* and *originality* in their responses to a problem. Flexibility is a measure of children's ability to use a variety of different methods or approaches to the problem; fluency is a measure of the number of appropriate solutions produced; and originality is a measure of the relative novelty of those responses (Haylock 1987).

Despite the tendency for mathematics to be viewed as a subject with a set body of knowledge, where algorithms and the search for 'the right' answer' are paramount, what the body of work on divergent thinking suggests is that being creative is more than the ability to solve problems. An important distinction to be made here is between procedural and conceptual understanding. Procedural knowledge relates to the extent to which children show computational accuracy, whereas conceptual knowledge is characterized by an understanding of how and why those computations work. This dichotomy is also reflected in Pólya's (1981) distinction between mathematical *information* and mathematical *know-how*, respectively. A child can solve a mathematical problem by correctly applying a learned algorithm without having any real conceptual understanding of how that answer came to be. Having some degree of conceptual understanding alongside the procedural competence allows the child much greater scope to show their mathematical creativity. It seems plausible to suggest that the ability to be mathematically creative comes from a sound knowledge base but this is not a sufficient criterion for mathematical creativity. What is also necessary is the ability to break free from the established way of doing things and the ability to apply this sound knowledge base to see opportunities beyond the given (Krutetskii 1976; Cropley 1992; Haylock 1997; Sriraman 2009). That is, being able to break free from the usual way of doing things and being able to show flexibility in one's approach to problem solving is where the real creativity lies.

Fixation in patterns of thought and then behaviour is seen to be the antithesis of the flexibility mentioned above and so breaking free from such fixations is seen as a key indicator of mathematical creativity. Certainly, the research suggests that such fixations can be seriously detrimental to children's success when engaging in problem solving. Haylock (1997) relates this to the four-stage process that eventually leads to mathematical creativity and invention as set out by the likes of Poincaré (1952) and Hadamard (1954). This four-stage process consists of *preparation* (which often involves working on and becoming familiar with a particular problem for some time without making any progress), *incubation* (which represents a period where the problem is put aside whilst other problems occupy the mind), *illumination* (where some and often sudden insight into the problem is gained), and *verification* (which involves confirming that the insight is correct). Haylock hypothesizes that the success in moving from the stage of incubation to illumination is the ability to show flexibility and break free from fixations of thought and that failure in problem solving can be seen in terms of the problem solver's thinking being fixated along inappropriate lines (Haylock 1997).

Most teachers are likely to have experienced children showing fixation at some point, as when they try to use a previously learned algorithm to complete a problem when the algorithm is not the best choice of approaches. A particularly useful example comes from the National Numeracy Project, which was set up in the UK in 1996 (Straker 1999). One of the arithmetic problems it used to assess children's ability to calculate mentally was 3000 − 1997. Surprisingly, only 31 per cent of the 10-year-olds involved in the project answered this question correctly. A subsequent analysis of the children's attempts at this question revealed that many of them failed because they were attempting to use the traditional vertical algorithm for subtraction when it would have been easier to use a more informal approach (e.g. counting on mentally or using a number line). That is, the failure was due to the children's fixation on a previously learned algorithm even when it was inappropriate.

Being flexible in problem solving is by no means the only way of being mathematically creative. Being allowed opportunities to pose problems can also lead to children showing their mathematical creativity (Silver 1997).

Teachers' conceptions of creativity

As pointed out in Chapter 1, research from around the world suggests that teachers' conceptions of creativity appear very similar, at least at a general level. Teachers tend to view creative children as *artistic, imaginative and inventive*. There continues to be a debate about whether a teacher's practice is directly influenced by the conception they have of the subject they are teaching (whether consciously or unconsciously held). Rene Thom was a firm believer in the idea that conceptions did impact on a teacher's practice in the classroom. He wrote that 'whether one wishes it or not, all mathematical pedagogy, even if scarcely coherent, rests on a philosophy of mathematics' (Thom 1973: 204). Still other studies have found little relationship between teachers' conceptions of the nature of mathematics and their teaching (e.g. Schraw and Olafson 2002). Others find that such beliefs shape classroom strategies (e.g. Lerman 1983; Thompson 1984; Hofer and Pintrich 1997). The link between teachers' conceptions of mathematics and their practices is therefore neither direct nor simple, but is mediated by a number of other factors, including the pressure to cover content, a lack of teaching experience, preferred teaching approaches and student reactions to them (Fryer and Collings 1991; Askew *et al.* 1997; Bolden 2006; Bolden and Newton 2008).

Furthermore, when teachers are asked about their general conceptions of creativity, these are unlikely to be sufficiently specific to have any significant impact on their teaching. However, when asked about conceptions of creativity at a more specific level, a level which ties it to their teaching, then there is likely to be a closer relationship between conceptions and teaching (e.g. Strauss 1993; Beswick 2004). This is important because a teacher who does not view their subject as creative is unlikely to promote it in his or her classroom. Strauss (1993) points out that teachers need to consider such beliefs and, if necessary, address them. On this basis, teachers' conceptions of what counts as creative thinking on the part of his or her pupils in the primary mathematics classroom can matter, and knowledge of these notions has the potential to be useful to pre-service teachers, serving teachers and teacher educators.

Teachers' conceptions of creativity in mathematics

Research has shown that mathematics is often viewed as a subject which offers few opportunities for pupils' creativity (Pehkonen 1997; Davies *et al.* 2004). Although teachers of primary-aged children often claim to believe that the mathematics in their classrooms is creative, closer inspection of their practices suggests that it is not. Instead, what the teachers involved seem to be referring to is the opportunities their mathematics sessions provide for creative teaching such as the creative use of resources and activities, for example, activities involving role play, construction, art, and songs and rhymes, rather than for creative thought in mathematics itself (Worthington and Carruthers 2003; Carruthers and Worthington 2005). Mann (2006) argues that the current way in which the teaching of mathematics is approached by many teachers only serves to stifle creativity. Even where students have met targets (like assessment goals) their learning experiences continue to be more of the same thing in many situations. Arguing for opportunities for creative thinking for pupils, he goes on to say: 'If mathematical talent is to be discovered and developed, changes in classroom practices and curricular materials are necessary. These changes will only be effective if creativity in mathematics is allowed to be part of the educational experience' (Mann 2006: 237).

There is also evidence that this occurs elsewhere in the world. A recent study from the USA shows that serving teachers hold misconceptions of what counts as creative behaviour and that this actually means they suppress children's creative behaviour in favour of non-creative behaviour (Skiba *et al.* 2010). Certainly, teachers of older children have been found routinely to dismiss creative thought (Kennedy 2005), particularly in subjects like mathematics, where they may view procedural competence as more important and creativity is seen as a distraction from that main aim of the lesson (Beghetto 2007).

A recent UK study exploring pre-service primary teachers' conceptions of creativity in mathematics asked teachers' views about whether mathematics was a creative subject and whether other subjects were more or less creative than mathematics (Bolden, Harries and Newton 2010). The results showed that the vast majority of teachers thought mathematics was not a creative subject and that most other subject domains offered more opportunities for creativity in the classroom. As has been indicated in past research, the teachers tended to have an arts-based bias where creativity was concerned. Subjects like English and art were seen as offering many more opportunities for creativity but even science was deemed to have greater scope for creativity than mathematics (see e.g. Newton and Newton 2009).

Semi-structured interviews were used to explore more deeply teachers' conceptions of creativity in mathematics as well as the reasons for expressing the views outlined above. In general, teachers held narrow and absolutist views of mathematics as a subject and the data suggested that most conceived mathematics as a subject with a set body of knowledge. Arts-based subjects and even subjects like science were perceived by teachers as offering much more scope for discussion, exploration of ideas and freedom of choice, involved greater use of the imagination and had fewer set goals and no correct answer. Encouraging creativity and assessing creativity in mathematics was also generally considered to be a difficult thing to do.

The pre-service teachers were also asked to think of a mathematics lesson that was creative and say something about what it was that made it creative. Teachers' views here fell into two broad categories; creativity as creative teaching and creativity as creative learning.

Creativity as creative teaching comprised two sub-categories: the teacher's imaginative use of resources and technology to teach the mathematics, and the way in which the teacher applied the mathematics to everyday examples. What is striking here is that both of these conceptions of creativity view it as something that resides predominantly with the teacher rather than the learner. This relates to the distinction made between teaching creatively and teaching for creativity, and illustrates that teachers' views of creativity tend to reflect the first of these two. Furthermore, the teachers' responses in the first of these categories (the imaginative use of resources and technology) related to the children having fun with the resources with little real consideration of the way in which the resources mentioned might have limitations or actually enhance the learning of mathematical concepts (i.e. there was little sense that teachers viewed the resources as representational tools with which children could be given better access to the mathematics involved). It is important to recognize that resources have limitations. For example, whilst number fans are an excellent resource to help young children see how numbers are built up in our base-10 system, they are difficult to use to perform calculations on numbers. For this, other resources are valuable. Thus, there is a need to understand the limitations of the resource being used.

The second broad category identified by the teachers concerned the way in which children constructed their own learning. There were two sub-categories here: the type of activity experienced and the development of flexibility in performing calculations. The first of these viewed creativity as children undertaking practical activities and investigations in the classroom. In these activities, there are no set ways of working, and so children are able to develop their own methods for approaching problems and are encouraged to explore ideas rather than just converge on an answer. Certain mathematical topics were perceived by teachers to offer more opportunities for creative learning in this respect. For example, shape, space and measures, fractions, division and data gathering were all identified as providing opportunities for the pupils to use their creativity while learning. Comments made by teachers here suggested they viewed active learning as important and something to be encouraged, but again, it was less clear the way in which the teachers saw the activities as helping to give children access to the meaning of the concepts. For example, although pizza slices might help to illustrate the 'part–whole' idea of fractions, whether it can be extended to help children to see fractions as numbers and whether it helps to give meaning to calculations with fractions was less clear.

The other sub-category within the larger second broad category related to children constructing their own learning was concerned with children developing computational flexibility. Teachers' comments here suggested a move away from a convergent view of mathematics, where a specific algorithm is learnt in order to obtain an answer to a more divergent view of mathematics where teachers encourage children to see mathematics as more open. Also important was the feeling that the way in which calculations are performed is at least as interesting as the answer. This suggested that the teachers viewed flexibility as a key element of creativity and as such this view of creativity is much more closely aligned with the view of creativity set out in earlier sections of this chapter. However, the origin of this aspect of creativity was not clear. Although teachers saw this flexibility as representing some degree of creativity in pupils, they also saw it as representing creativity in teachers, in the sense that it is the teacher who initially offers children a variety of computational methods. This relates to creativity as creative teaching, discussed earlier.

The sample of pre-service teachers involved in the above study was relatively small (38) and self-selected, and although the authors did not suggest that the teacher conceptions identified represented an exhaustive taxonomy, the teachers were thought typical of many other primary teachers in the UK. For instance, most had not studied mathematics beyond GCSE/GCE 'O' level. Consequently, the findings are likely to resonate with other teachers' and their conceptions of creativity, and therefore are relatable to other groups of teachers and contexts [see Bassey (2001) for a discussion of the 'relatability' of research findings]. As such the findings from this and other studies involving teachers' conceptions of mathematics raise a number of concerns for the teaching and learning of the subject. First, if teachers' conceptions of a subject influence their subsequent practice in the classroom, then such teachers are not likely to value creativity in young children. In fact, the research suggests they may not even recognize it (Skiba *et al.* 2010). The real danger is that they may actually suppress children's mathematical creativity.

What was also interesting about the research described above (Bolden *et al.* 2010) was that teachers' narrow conceptions of mathematics were found to be the result of the way in which they themselves had experienced mathematics during their own schooling, which was often laden with negative feelings. If teachers teach the way they themselves were taught or, as discussed earlier, their narrow conceptions shape their pedagogy, then they are likely to simply perpetuate the cycle of mathematics as a body of sterile facts to be learned which are unrelated to the real world. This will simply lead to a new generation of children who experience mathematics the same way, and so the cycle will continue. What is rather depressing is that research from the USA suggests that teachers of mathematics do not value unique comments made by children in class and actually emphasize memorization over creativity in the mistaken belief that it will prepare children for future learning (Beghetto 2007, 2008).

Fostering creativity in the primary mathematics classroom

Teachers, both in the UK and in other countries, are being urged to foster creativity in young children across all curriculum subjects, including mathematics [National Advisory Committee on Creative and Cultural Education (NACCCE) 1999; Office for Standards in Education (Ofsted) 2003; Department for Education and Skills (DfES) 2003; DfES/ Department for Culture, Media and Sport (DCMS) 2006; Qualifications and Curriculum Development Agency (QCDA) 2008]. However, there appears to be a dearth of information concerning how teachers might encourage children to be creative and use real problem-solving skills and strategies (Makel 2009). In the UK, the government introduced online resources to help teachers make sense of what this means across the different subject domains (QCDA 2008). This site offers pre-service and serving teachers a number of case studies which illustrate how teachers may encourage children to be creative in a variety of subject domains. Unfortunately, mathematics is only conspicuous by its absence here. It is not surprising then that teachers should ask what experiences and opportunities they should offer in the primary mathematics classroom to help children develop their creativity. The following section attempts to provide some answers to this question.

The discussion above concerning Guildford's (1967) distinction between convergent and divergent thinking suggests that pupils should be encouraged to develop their mathematical creativity by being offered activities that are open-ended and have multiple solutions. Kwon, Park and Park (2006) developed a programme aimed at encouraging divergent thinking in primary-aged children via open-ended tasks and discovered that their use was indeed helpful in developing mathematical creativity (as measured by *fluency*, *flexibility* and *originality*). Providing children with opportunities for open-ended problem solving, which can emphasize divergent thinking, is facilitated by that aspect of the National Curriculum in England called Using and Applying Mathematics. This was once a separate entity but more recently the expectation is that it should pervade all aspects of children's mathematics. Even so, it is not likely to be as easy for teachers as it might appear, as encouraging divergent thinking requires teachers to have confidence in their own mathematical ability and to break away from the usual way of doing things (i.e. using closed or convergent problems). It also requires time, something which teachers seem to lack (see Bolden and Newton 2008). However, only by providing children with open-ended problem-solving opportunities can we hope to develop children's fluency, flexibility and originality in problem-solving and thus the ability to break free from established mind sets (Haylock 1987; Silver 1997; Mann 2006).

Asking pupils to reason through their mathematics and to communicate this reasoning to others is another way in which children can be encouraged to develop their mathematical creativity. The teacher can aid this process by using questioning that is open-ended rather than closed and which demands pupils to go beyond the answer and to demonstrate their reasoning (Sheffield 2009). Encouraging pupils to ask themselves questions that may extend their thinking can also be fruitful in this respect. Silver (1997) suggests that problem posing as well as problem solving can be associated with mathematical creativity in school. In developing a programme to develop children's mathematical creativity, Sheffield suggests pupils should be encouraged to extend their mathematical explorations by asking questions concerning *who* (can re-state this in their own words?), *what* (patterns/generalizations do I see?), *when* (does this work or not work?), *where* (could I go next?), *why* (does that work?) and *how* (does this relate to real life?). Recent work suggests that children trained in such techniques not only strengthen their mathematical creativity but also improve their general mathematical abilities compared to children not trained (Sheffield 2009).

It is important to note that developing an appropriate classroom ethos is crucial in encouraging young children's creativity in mathematics. An ethos where questioning and risk-taking are encouraged and mistakes are viewed as potential pathways to greater understanding rather than outcomes to be avoided at all costs will help greatly in this respect.

Giving more control of what takes place in the classroom to pupils can also be a productive strategy to adopt. This need not be limited to just the content of the mathematics but can extend to assessment too. Involving pupils in self- and peer-assessment of their own work can act as assessment and learning. Assessment drives what we teach so it is important that, if we value creativity in mathematics, then we need to become creative in the way we assess. That is, creative assessment is likely to require an understanding of what children know rather than what they don't know and this will need to look very different from the modes of assessment than we currently have in operation in the National Curriculum in England. When knowing is viewed as an understanding of the overarching principles of a subject domain, then assessment practices will need to assess that understanding across a wider range of the domain, which means assessments will need to be larger in their scope.

The list below offers the teacher of primary mathematics some general principles for developing creative thinking in their pupils.

- Question your own approach to mathematics (i.e. can it be creative or is it about memorizing rules?).

■ Empower the learner (e.g. by encouraging a 'have a go' ethos in your classroom where mistakes/misconceptions are embraced as teaching and learning opportunities, by involving them in deciding on the mathematics to be learned, by asking them to problem pose not just problem solve).

■ Allow children to 'discover' the mathematics rather than always setting out the learning objective at the beginning of the lesson.

■ Embrace 'open-endedness', that is, use more open-ended problems with multiple solutions rather than closed problems, and use more open-ended questions that require children to think about their answer rather than a closed question that requires a closed response, or a yes/no or definitive answer.

■ Encourage children to reason through their ideas and answers. Use the *'who, what, when, where, why, how'* approach.

■ Above all, try to instil in your children the feeling that mathematics is an activity that can be fun.

Summary

This chapter has argued that mathematics in the primary classroom can be characterized by both teacher and pupil creativity and not just as an activity involving a sterile and closed body of facts involving memorization of algorithms. It has also set out research suggesting that teachers' conceptions of creativity in mathematics are often rather narrow and often the product of the way they themselves were taught. This means that teachers can often fail to spot creativity when they see it in young children. We need to break this cycle. Highlighting these findings to those involved in teacher education or in continuing professional development is one way of beginning this process. Another is to offer primary teachers of mathematics some examples of how children's creativity can be encouraged, and this chapter has attempted to do just that. If we adopt some of the suggestions outlined above, then recent research suggests that many pupils are likely to benefit, both in terms of their ability to be mathematically creative and in their all-round mathematical ability. It may also begin to alter the often distorted way in which pupils view mathematics and see it not as described above but rather as an open body of developing knowledge which represents a beautiful and exciting way of viewing and thinking about the world. The question then becomes not whether we can encourage mathematical creativity in young children but whether we can afford not to.

References

Askew, M., Brown, M., Rhodes, V., Johnson, D. and William, W. (1997) *Effective Teachers of Numeracy: Report of a study carried out for the Teacher Training Agency*, London: King's College London.

Bassey, M. (2001) 'A solution to the problem of generalization in educational research: Fuzzy prediction', *Oxford Review of Education*, 22(1): 5–22.

Beghetto, R.A. (2007) 'Does creativity have a place in classroom discussions? Teachers' response preferences', *Thinking Skills and Creativity*, 2(1): 1–9.

Beghetto, R.A. (2008) 'Prospective teachers' beliefs about imaginative thinking in K-12 schooling', *Thinking Skills and Creativity*, 3: 134–42.

Beswick, K. (2004) 'The impact of teachers' perceptions of student characteristics on the enactment of their beliefs', in M.J. Høines and A.B. Fuglestad (eds) *Proceedings of the 28th Conference of the International Group for the Psychology of Mathematics Education*, Vol. 2, Bergen: Bergen University College, pp. 111–18.

Boden, M.A. (2004) *The Creative Mind – Myths and Mechanisms*, London: Routledge.

Bolden, D.S. (2006) *Primary Teachers' Epistemological Beliefs about the Teaching and Learning of Mathematics: The link with and implications for their classroom pedagogy*. Unpublished doctoral thesis, University of Durham.

Bolden, D.S., Harries, A.V. and Newton, D.P. (2010) 'Pre-service primary teachers' conceptions of creativity in mathematics', *Educational Studies in Mathematics*, 73: 143–57.

Bolden, D.S. and Newton, L.D. (2008) 'Primary teachers' epistemological beliefs: some perceived barriers to investigative teaching in primary mathematics', *Educational Studies*, 34(5): 419–32.

Carruthers, E. and Worthington, M. (2005) 'Making sense of mathematical graphics: The development of understanding abstract symbolism', *European Childhood Research Journal*, 13(1): 57–79.

Cockroft, W.H. (1982) *Mathematics Counts: Report of the Committee of Inquiry into the Teaching of Mathematics in Schools*, London: HMSO.

Craft, A. (2002) *Creativity and Early Years Education*. London: Continuum.

Craft, A. (2003) 'The limits of creativity in education: Dilemmas for the educator', *British Journal of Educational Studies*, 51(2): 113–27.

Cropley, A.J. (1992) *More Ways than One: Fostering Creativity*, New Jersey: Ablex.

Csikszentmihalyi, M. (1996) *Creativity: Flow and the psychology of discovery and invention*, New York: HarperCollins.

Davies, D., Howe, A., Rogers, M. and Fasciato, M. (2004) 'How do trainee primary teachers understand creativity?' in E. Norman, D. Spendlove, P. Grover and A. Mitchell (eds) *Creativity and Innovation – Proceedings of the DATA International Research Conference 2004*, Wellesbourne: The Design and Technology Association.

Department for Education and Skills (DfES) (2003) *Excellence and Enjoyment*. London: DfES.

Department for Education and Skills/Department for Culture, Media and Sport (DfES/DCMS) (2006) *Nurturing Creativity in Young People*, London: DfES/DCMS.

Diakidoy, I.-A.N. and Kanari, E. (1999) 'Student teachers' beliefs about creativity', *British Educational Research Journal*, 25(2): 225–43.

Fryer, M. and Collings, J.A. (1991) 'Teachers' views about creativity', *British Journal of Educational Psychology*, 61: 207–19.

Gruber, H.E. and Wallace, D.B. (2000) 'The case study method and evolving systems approach for understanding unique creative people at work', in R.J. Sternberg (ed.) *Handbook of Creativity*, Cambridge: Cambridge University Press, pp. 93–115.

Guildford, I.P. (1967) 'Creativity: Yesterday, today, and tomorrow', *Journal of Creative Behaviour*, 1: 3–14.

Hadamard, J. (1954) *The Psychology of Invention in the Mathematical Field*, New York: Dover Publications.

Haylock, D. (1987) 'A framework for assessing mathematical creativity in schoolchildren', *Educational Studies in Mathematics*, 18(1): 59–74.

Haylock, D. (1997) 'Recognizing mathematical creativity in schoolchildren', *International Journal on Mathematical Education*, 29(3): 68–74.

Hofer, B.K. and Pintrich, P.R. (1997) 'The development of epistemological theories: Beliefs about knowledge and knowing and their relation to learning', *Review of Educational Research*, 67: 88–140.

Kennedy, M. (2005) *Inside Teaching: How classroom life undermines reform*, Cambridge, MA: Harvard University Press.

Kwon, O.H., Park, J.S. and Park, J.S. (2006) 'Cultivating divergent thinking in mathematics through an open-ended approach', *Asia-Pacific Education Review*, 7(1): 51–61.

Krutetskii, V.A. (1976) *The Psychology of Mathematical Abilities in Schoolchildren*, Chicago: University of Chicago Press.

Leikin, R. (2009) 'Exploring mathematical creativity using multiple solution tasks', in R. Leikin, A. Berman, and B. Koichu (eds) *Creativity in Mathematics and the Education of Gifted Students*, Rotterdam: Sense Publishers, pp. 129–46.

Lerman, S. (1983) 'Problem solving or knowledge centred: The influence of philosophy on mathematics teaching', *International Journal of Mathematical Education in Science and Technology*, 14(1): 59–66.

Makel, M.C. (2009) 'Help us creativity researchers, you're our only hope', *Psychology of Aesthetics, Creativity and the Arts*, 3: 38–42.

Mann, E.L. (2006) 'Creativity: The essence of mathematics', *Journal for the Education of the Gifted*, 30(2): 236–60.

National Advisory Committee on Creative and Cultural Education (NACCCE) (1999) *All Our Futures: Creativity, culture and education*, London: Department for Education and Employment.

Newton, D.P. and Newton, L.D. (2009) 'Some student teachers' conceptions of creativity in school science', *Research in Science and Technological Education*, 27(1): 45–60.

Office for Standards in Education (Ofsted) (2003) *Expecting the Unexpected: Developing creativity in primary and secondary schools*, London: Ofsted.

Pehkonen, E. (1997) 'The state-of-art in mathematical creativity', *International Journal on Mathematical Education*, 29(3): 63–7.

Plucker, J.A., Beghetto, R.A. and Dow, G.T. (2004) 'Why isn't creativity more important to educational psychologists? Potential, pitfalls, and future directions in creativity research', *Educational Psychologist*, 39: 83–96.

Poincaré, H. (1952) *Science and Method*, New York: Dover Publications.

Pólya, G. (1981) *Mathematical Discovery*, Chichester: John Wiley.

Qualifications and Curriculum Development Agency (QCDA) (2008) *Learning Across the Curriculum – Creativity*. Online. Available at: http://webarchive.nationalarchives.gov.uk/20100823130703/http://curriculum.qcda.gov.uk/key-stages-1-and-2/learning-across-the-curriculum/creativity/index.aspx (accessed 14 February 2010).

Schraw, G. and Olafson, L. (2002) 'Teachers' epistemological world views and educational practices', *Issues in Education: Contributions from Educational Psychology*, 8(2): 99–148.

Sheffield, L.J. (2009) 'Developing mathematical creativity – questions may be the answer', in R. Leikin, A. Berman and B. Koichu (eds) *Creativity in Mathematics and the Education of Gifted Students*, Rotterdam: Sense Publishers, pp. 87–100.

Silver, E.A. (1997) 'Fostering creativity through instruction rich in mathematical problem solving and problem posing', *ZDM*, 29(3): 75–80.

Skiba, T., Tan, M. Sternberg, R.J. and Grigorenko, E.L. (2010) 'Roads not taken, new roads to take: Looking for creativity in the classroom', in R.A. Beghetto and J.C. Kaufman (eds) *Nurturing Creativity in the Classroom*, New York: Cambridge University Press, pp. 252–69.

Sriraman, B. (2005) 'Are giftedness and creativity synonyms in mathematics?' *The Journal of Secondary Gifted Education*, 27(1): 20–36.

Sriraman, B. (ed.) (2008) *Creativity, Giftedness, and Talent Development in Mathematics*, Charlotte, NC: Information Age Publishing, Inc.

Sriraman, B. (2009) 'The characteristics of mathematical creativity', *ZDM: The International Journal on Mathematics Education*, 41: 13–27.

Sternberg, R.J. (ed.) (1988) *The Nature of Creativity: Contemporary Psychological Perspectives*, New York: Cambridge University Press.

Straker, A. (1999) 'The National Numeracy Project: 1996–1999', in I. Thompson (ed.), *Issues in Teaching Numeracy in Primary Schools*, Buckingham: Open University Press, pp. 39–48.

Strauss, S. (1993) 'Teachers' pedagogical content knowledge about children's minds and learning: Implications for teacher education', *Educational Psychologist*, 28: 279–90.

Thom, R. (1973) 'Modern mathematics: does it exist?', in A.G. Howson (ed.) *Developments in Mathematical Education*, Cambridge: Cambridge University Press, pp. 194–209.

Thompson, A.G. (1984) 'The relationship of teachers' conceptions of mathematics and mathematics teaching to instructional practice', *Educational Studies in Mathematics*, 15: 105–27.

Torrance, E.P. (1974) *Torrance Tests of Creative Thinking*, Bensenville, IL: Scholastic Testing Service.

Weisberg, R.W. (1988) 'Problem solving and creativity', in R.J. Sternberg (ed.) *The Nature of Creativity*, Cambridge: Cambridge University Press, pp. 148–76.

Worthington, M. and Carruthers, E. (2003) *Children's Mathematics: Making marks, making meaning*, London: Paul Chapman.

Creativity in Science and Design and Technology

Lynn Newton

Introduction

One of the pleasures of teaching is in the creative opportunities it presents, both for the teacher and for the learner. A lesson, personally crafted for the occasion, taught with interest and enthusiasm, resulting in understanding and creative thought on the part of the pupils, is hugely satisfying and motivating. The ability to craft such a lesson needs a teacher who does not follow blindly the plans of others, who knows what the subject is about, who understands the science and who recognizes the opportunities for creative thinking. What are these opportunities?

The notion of creativity in science and design and technology

It was not until the twentieth century that people generally began to link the words *creativity* and *science*. But where is the creativity in doing science? Klahr and Dunbar (1998) described two thinking spaces involved in doing science. The first is in the *hypothesis space*, where tentative descriptions and causal explanations are constructed. The second is in the *experiment space*, where ways of collecting information and evaluating these tentative explanations are constructed. To these may be added a third, the *application space*, in which scientific (and other) knowledge is used to solve practical problems, an aspect of endeavour commonly described as technology (Newton and Newton 2009a). Each of these involves imagination to generate ideas and construct alternative, possible worlds: in essence, 'What if …?' thinking. This imagination, however, is not free to be wild, wacky or weird, but is constrained by what counts as appropriate in science and in technology. So, in science, a tentative explanation of some event or phenomenon has to be at least scientifically plausible or believable and, preferably, simple or elegant. In technology, a potential solution to a practical problem has to function or be fit for purpose and, preferably simple or elegant. Note, however, that the constraints on imagination in science and technology are not quite the same. A scientist might give roughly equal weight to novelty, plausibility and elegance, but a technologist is likely to give priority to function.

In the primary school

In the school curriculum, science and technology may be separate domains of skills, knowledge and understanding as in England [Qualifications and Curriculum Authority (QCA) 2008]. It is possible to distinguish between the two. For example, creativity in science is popularly called 'discovery', while creativity on the application of science to meet needs and solve problems is popularly called 'invention' (Hadamard 1954). There will be times, however, when a teacher may integrate the two of them so that the science moves smoothly into a practical problem for the children to solve or begins with a practical problem which requires study in science to solve it. Indeed, in some countries, like Scotland, science and technology may be presented as one in the school curriculum [Scottish Executive Education Department (SEED) 2006]. At all times, however, a teacher will need to be aware that what counts as worthwhile creative thought in the two domains may not be entirely the same. The teacher must also allow for the age and experience of the child. Osborne *et al.* (2001: 17) in their discussion of creativity as one of the nine themes in science teaching, recognized that such a theme is not easy to teach explicitly but argued that it was still important for teachers to try to offer pupils 'opportunities to be genuinely creative ... [to] do science, rather than being taught about creativity ... and to consider possible ideas to explain phenomena and test hypotheses'. Because young children lack the knowledge and experience that would make it possible, it is very unlikely that any primary aged child could be truly creative like a scientist. However, they have the potential to develop and show creativity in the hypothesis space (making sense of the world), the experiment space (collecting and evaluating scientific evidence) and the application space (solving practical problems). Depending on the children's prior knowledge and amount of teacher's help, these ideas would be more or less new to them. The ideas might also be applied in creative thought in the application space when they are asked to solve a problem or construct something, like a warning system using their knowledge of circuits and buzzers. They might also, for example, have opportunities to synthesize scientific information about the moon to construct an account of what it would be like to live there, or they might construct an analogy to describe what is going on when a hot, wet tea-towel is hung on a washing line on a cold morning, or they might make a connection between a prism, a raindrop and a rainbow.

But what does this creative thought look like in the primary science classroom? Table 4.1 identifies the key fields of scientific creativity and associated behaviours.

When thinking in the *hypothesis space*, children have opportunities to be creative when they are asked to *construct more or less tentative descriptions* of, for instance, properties, scenarios, trends and patterns, structural models and analogies. For example, a younger primary child notices a pattern in some presented data on how bigger children seem to be able to hold their breath for longer; older children use scientific information to imagine living on a space station or describe a cross-section through the Earth as being like cutting open a peach. An extension of this involves the children in *constructing more or less tentative explanations* involving, for example, reasons, causes, hypotheses, theories,

TABLE 4.1 Fields of scientific creative thought

SCIENTIFIC CREATIVITY	BEHAVIOUR
Field 1: Making scientific sense of the world	Opportunities for children's creative thought are afforded by extending or articulating descriptive and explanatory understandings to produce new possibilities
Field 2: Gathering and evaluating scientific information and evidence	Usually referred to as 'experiments' or 'practical investigations', opportunities for pupils' creative thinking comes from the generation of ideas and ways to test them
Field 3: Applying science in new contexts	Opportunities for creative thought are cast in the form of problems to solve or challenges

functional models and analogies. For example, a younger child explains why the water in the pond has frozen; an older primary child thinks of a reason for why a drinking straw looks bent in a glass of water, or connects the way a ball bounces off side cushions in table billiards with light rays reflecting from shiny surfaces.

In the *experiment space*, children have opportunities to use creative thought when they are asked to *construct a practical way to find reliable, descriptive information*. For example, a younger child suggests a way to see whether different shoe soles make a difference on slippery surfaces; older pupils design a test to see if sound travels through water. Taking their thinking further in the experiment space, they might be asked to *construct a practical way to test a tentative explanation of an observation or event*, for example, younger children suggest a way to test their idea that not all things made from metal stick to magnets; an older child devises a practical investigation to see if 'light for its size' is what matters for things which float.

Thinking in the *application space*, children have opportunities to be creative when they are asked to apply their ideas in new contexts and solve practical problems. For example, younger children use their knowledge of the properties of materials to make a waterproof roof for a doll's house; older pupils apply their knowledge of electric circuits to put some lights on a card tree.

Of course, opportunities in these fields are not mutually exclusive. For example, a child may extrapolate from observations to arrive at a causal explanation as when he speculates that shoes with studs will have more grip than those without studs. He might revise an explanation after examining the results as when he decides that more wheels do not make a toy car go faster.

On this basis, there are opportunities in primary school science for children to exercise creative scientific thought and action. Science is not all about facts and figures: is it a subject in which children can create their own understandings and ways of putting those to the test. In technology, there is the opportunity to use these and other understandings in solving practical problems. Of course, science lessons offer other opportunities for productive activities, such making models, painting pictures and writing poems, but these do not necessarily exercise creative *scientific* thought.

Teachers' conceptions of creativity in science and technology

In the context of science, while some researchers have found little relationship between teachers' conceptions of aspects of science and their teaching (e.g. Duschl and Wright 1989; Mellado 1997), others have found the opposite – that such beliefs determine classroom strategies (e.g. Pajares 1992; Hofer and Pintrich 1997; Waters-Adams 2006). It is likely that this difference in the research findings is because the link between teachers' conceptions of science and their classroom practices is complex, mediated by matters like the pressure on teachers to cover content, a lack of teaching experience, preferred teaching approaches and student reactions to them (Fryer and Collings 1991; Brickhouse and Bodner 1992; Bell *et al.* 2000). Furthermore, when teachers' conceptions are accessed at the general level, the responses are likely to be too vague to shape planning and teaching. With other subjects when accessed at the specific level, however, there tends to be a closer relationship between conceptions and teaching (e.g. Strauss 1993; Lunn 2002; Beswick 2004).

If creativity is not perceived to have a place in a subject's teaching, it is unlikely to be included in a teacher's goals. At the general level, teachers' beliefs about creativity in different parts of the world are similar, with some subjects seen as offering fewer opportunities for creative thought than others, science being one of them. For example, Dickinson *et al.* (2000: 12) found pre-service teachers in the USA believed that 'there is no creativity after data collection because a scientist has to be objective'. In Canada, Aguirre *et al.* (1990) found them to believe that creativity and imagination were unimportant in science. In the UK, primary teachers were found to have a narrow, arts-based view of creativity, with science seen as relatively uncreative (Davies *et al.* 2004).

New teachers' views

While exploring conceptions of creativity in primary science, pre-service primary teachers were asked to rank the subjects of the primary curriculum in order of the opportunities for creative thinking they provided (Newton and Newton 2009b). These new teachers all believed that science lessons offer some opportunities for creative thought, but subjects like art, drama and music offered significantly more, as did technology with its opportunities for problem solving. When asked why they thought this, their reasons indicated that these areas of the curriculum: were more open-ended, were less theoretical, involved less writing, were more open to self-expression, allowed independent activity, encouraged imagination, and did not require 'right' answers. On the other hand, science, along with history, was seen as offering more opportunities than subjects like modern foreign languages, geography, mathematics and religious education. In the latter subjects, the new teachers felt that pupils were told what to do more and the emphasis was on the acquisition of facts and following patterns and rules. All tended to think that arts-related subjects provide more opportunities for creative thought than other subjects. Their emphasis was 'more' rather than 'different' and, given their views, this is of concern because of the way conceptions can shape practice. Those who do not feel confident enough in their own understanding of science to explain or draw out explanations from the children are likely to play safe in their lessons, filling them with facts-focused activities and avoiding reasons. Investigative work given to the children will lack a press for meaning or creative thinking. Other teachers might actually believe that science *is* about facts and descriptions, and emphasize and give marks for these. Consequently, they may provide little or no opportunity for understanding and creativity on the part of the pupils. For them science lessons will amount to learning the words and descriptions, a misconception reinforced by some government-managed assessment processes.

The inherent danger here is that this, in turn, will shape the pupils' conceptions. A consequence of this is a decline in interest in science, as described by Bore (2006) in her discussion of the two challenges facing science educators today. The first focuses on the need for teachers to address the increasing dissatisfaction of pupils with science as they move into adolescence. She describes how this dissatisfaction is not unique to England and focuses on school science being seen by many pupils internationally as irrelevant to everyday life. This need not be the case: science *is* relevant but its relevance is not necessarily being made explicit by teachers when teaching science (Newton 1989). The second challenge, according to Bore, is the downturn in learning noted as pupils move from primary to secondary school. Braund and Driver (2005) drew on the work of others to suggest this regression in learning is the result of a disjunction between phases (primary and secondary) and noted that the evidence suggests this was a problem internationally. More significantly, they also identified that this down turn in learning is most marked in science.

To determine conceptions of creativity at the specific primary science classroom level, the pre-service primary school teachers mentioned earlier were asked for specific examples of science topics and lessons in which children were being scientifically creative, how they would encourage creative thinking and what they saw as evidence of the presence or absence of scientifically creative thought (Newton and Newton 2009b). From the data, five categories of conception were identified (Table 4.2). There were two major

TABLE 4.2 Summary of pre-service teachers' categories of conceptions

CATEGORY	SUB-CATEGORY	EXAMPLE
1	1a) Students experience the world and generate explanations (Here, creativity is in the construction of a plausible casual explanation)	– The teacher provides direct experience of some scientific phenomenon and the children are asked to explain it (e.g. *Why do the bulbs go dimmer when you add more to a circuit?*)
	1b) Students experience the world, generate explanations and test (Here, creativity is in the generation of a test of their predictions and explanations)	– This extends sub-category 1a by asking the students to test their ideas through practical investigation (e.g. *The students use batteries, bulbs and wires to test whether their explanation holds true*)

CATEGORY	SUB-CATEGORY	EXAMPLE
2	Students use scientific information to imagine situations and events (Here, creativity is seen here as being use of imagination)	– Factual information is made more interesting, meaningful or memorable by providing experiences requiring students to use imagination to integrate them into existing understandings (e.g. *What would it be like living on the space station for 6 months?*)
3	3a) Students plan and carry out practical activities (investigations) to determine facts and answer given scientific questions (Here, creativity is in the designing process.)	– The focus is on designing ways to collect relevant information and data to answer factual questions, but no explanations are required (e.g. *What are the best gloves for keeping our hands warm in winter?*)
	3b) Students apply scientific knowledge to solve a given practical problem (Here, creativity is in the application of knowledge to generate possible solutions to the problem)	– Scientific knowledge is applied to solve a specific given problem (e.g. *Students are asked to find a way to stop the seedlings from drying out over the one-week holiday*)
	3c) Students carry out fact-finding practical activities and then apply what they have done to solve a given practical problem (Here, creativity is a combination of 3a and 3b)	– Practical investigation leads to drawing on factual information to generate solutions to problems that can be tried (e.g. *What material would be the best to use as an insulator to keep mountain climbers warm and dry?*)
4	Students' develop positive feelings about science during the lesson, perhaps through a novel or exciting demonstration or task – the 'wow!' factor (Here, creativity is largely to do with atmosphere and engagement)	– The science lesson is designed to surprise or excite the students, generating interest and motivation (e.g. *in a lesson on solids, liquids and gases, the children investigate how many burps there are in a bottle of fizzy lemonade*)
5	Students are doing or making things to consolidate an idea (Here, the creativity is less to do with creative thought on the part of the students and more creative teaching strategies)	– The teacher provides detailed instructions for the students to follow, to make the learning concrete, meaningful or memorable (e.g. *in the school hall the children act out the movement of the planets around the sun*)

Source: Newton and Newton, 2010b.

clusters – constructing tests of facts, and using science knowledge to solve a practical problem – and two lesser clusters were to do with making things, and constructing descriptions/explanations. Very few of the new teachers thought that the generation of an explanation was a creative activity. The majority focused on the experiment space but within that space, attention was largely on fact-finding with few including the testing of tentative explanations. Several added the application space. Others included making activities which followed detailed instructions and some included activities which were creative but in other subjects like drama and art. Overall, their conceptions were narrow and, at times, inappropriate.

Regarding encouraging creative thought, these new teachers said it was difficult to do. Their reasons were that creativity is hard to define, children of this age have an insufficient grasp of science to be creative in it, and children are not aware that they were allowed or expected to be creative. One interesting response was that the nature of science itself, 'which deals with the invisible', makes creativity in science difficult. Another was that creative thought was beyond the teacher's control. A small number said it depended on the child, the resources and the science topic. The most frequent reason for a lack of opportunity was that the topic did not provide much opportunity for practical work but some saw opportunities for practical work where others saw none. In addition, the trainees all indicated that they considered assessing creativity was a problem for them.

Experienced teachers' views

A group of experienced teachers was asked to rate a set of classroom activities for the extent to which they provided opportunity for creative thinking in science (Newton and Newton 2010a). Analysis of the results showed that, although there was variation amongst the teachers in their ability to discriminate between the incidents, all of them, broadly speaking, could distinguish between incidents offering more opportunity for scientific creativity and those offering more opportunity for scientific reproductive thought. Only a very few teachers showed little or no ability to discriminate between activities offering reproductive thought and those offering creative thought. There was, however, across the whole group, a tendency to favour fact-seeking practical work and the application of facts to solve practical problems. In addition, some teachers did not discriminate between scientific creative incidents and non-scientific creative incidents. Like the new teachers, many of the experienced teachers also considered that assessing creativity was a problem for them.

In the two studies described here, care was taken to explore conceptions at the specific level of classroom activity. Consequently, the responses are considered to indicate how teachers are likely to respond when urged to provide opportunities for scientifically creative thought in the primary classroom. In particular, they may neglect opportunities to be creative in the hypothesis space while favouring those in the experiment and application spaces, especially where these relate to fact-finding activities. Some teachers may also think that reproductive making activities and non-scientific creative activities carried out in the science classroom are scientifically creative (Newton and Newton 2010b). It may also be that, as a consequence, when trainee teachers are placed in schools for teaching practice they may not be well advised in this aspect of their work by the supervising teachers.

Fostering creative thinking and problem solving in science and technology

In England, one of the aims of the centrally controlled National Curriculum is for young people to be creative, resourceful and able to identify and solve problems (QCA 2008) and teachers are encouraged to provide experiences that enable pupils to become creative thinkers. Kind and Kind (2007) identify three key strategies and approaches that can support creative thinking: raising questions; providing open investigations; and, encouraging working with explanations. In a discussion of creativity as a motivational tool in science education to enhance cognitive engagement, Hoang (2007) suggests that teachers should encourage hands-on activity, whether individual or cooperative; give pupils control by giving them risk-free open-ended tasks; and increase exposure to creativity in cross-curricular contexts within science.

There are obviously overlaps between these suggestions and the goals of these science educators are not, of course, mutually exclusive. What follows synthesizes various ideas to show how creative thought might be encouraged and supported in the primary science classroom. While areas for opportunity are treated separately for convenience, it is recognized that there can be considerable overlap between them.

Scientific creativity in talk and questions

Jeffrey and Craft (2001) emphasize the social dimension of creativity – the interplay between individuals in a group, the development of coping strategies and individual empowerment, and the importance of risk balanced by confidence. The importance of structured interaction though class discussion is important. The crucial role of talk – teacher to pupil, pupil to teacher or pupil to pupil – should not be underestimated (see e.g. Newton 2008). From their work with primary pupils using puppets in science lessons to promote engagement and talk, Maloney et al. (n.d.) argue for the role of imaginative discussion. Activities and experiences that encourage children to describe and explain their ideas in science fit with the first field of scientific creativity discussed earlier.

One particular approach that encourages description and explanations is through questioning. According to Osborne et al. (2001:18), teachers see questioning as 'part and parcel of the process of science'. Most questions asked in a busy science classroom are to do with organization and management. Where they do focus on science, they tend to be factual or recall questions. For creative thinking, it is important to give pupils opportunities to ask '*Why …?*' '*What if …?*' and '*Could you …?*' questions. These questions focus attention and encourage the children to explain, apply their ideas in new contexts and create alternatives (Newton 1997). Focused questions can be selected to encourage understanding and creative thought.

Scientific creativity in play

Various kinds of talk, including discussion and questioning, can be encouraged through the use of imaginative play and games. The role of play in developing the creative abilities of young pupils is important (Beetlestone 1998; Craft 2002). Imaginative play is often voluntary, non-serious, enjoyable, satisfying and intrinsically valuable in terms of social, moral and emotional development. It also encourages imagination and creative thought. It tends to be associated with very young children and early years settings, but children can be involved in purposeful structured play right through primary school (and, indeed, beyond). Structured play through games that teachers provide allows children to make friends and learn to cooperate, explore ideas and events safely, develop and extend basic skills, and learn what is and is not acceptable – the rules of action and behaviour. It also supports cognitive development and in particular the development and use of thinking skills, including creative thought. Simultaneously, teachers are scaffolding the learning that is being demonstrated and developed. Amabile (2002) argues that to be creative people (and that includes young learners) need time for 'combinational play' where time pressures are avoided while opportunities for high levels of exploration, learning and idea generations are provided. This encourages imagination and reflection without the pressure to complete a task.

Various opportunities for structured play in science can be used to help children think creatively and solve problems. Table 4.3 shows some ideas for activities in science.

TABLE 4.3 Opportunities for creative thought in science lessons

FOCUS	OPPORTUNITIES/ACTIVITIES
Session starters/talk abouts	– Collections of toys or unusual or unfamiliar artefacts to stimulate question asking and answering, explanations and reasoning (e.g. old toys no longer available or seen today, automata, clockwork toys, objects that move in odd ways or make strange noises).
	– Pairs of pictures that are connected in some way; the children have to work out the links between them; have a range of difficulty; the connections could be causal or descriptive or explanatory (e.g. a picture of some guinea-pig food including sunflower seeds and a copy of Van Gogh's picture of sunflowers; a snowy road scene and a big truck on its side)
	– An assortment of photographs of plants, animals or scientific phenomena taken from unusual angles or perspectives, great distances or very close-up (e.g. the children notice features and details, use analogy and try to recognize them)
	– A feely box (e.g. a sealed box with a hole in the side into which the child puts his or her hand to feel what is inside; encourages the use of a different sense to generate description and explanation – 'I think it is … because …')

FOCUS	OPPORTUNITIES/ACTIVITIES
Role-play corners	– Many primary classrooms, especially those with younger children, will have general role-play corners, like a house or a shop. These are used to encourage social, language or mathematical skills. Try a scientifically focused role-play corner (e.g. a veterinary surgery, populated by various soft toys where the children can think about the care of animals; a space station where context can be explored; a garden centre allows children to think about seeds and seedlings, larger plants, and what plants need to grow)
Games/knitting ideas together	– Bingo (e.g. the children's cards have key words or ideas on them; the teacher gives the explanation and the children match it to the idea; later, the task is reversed, with the teacher stating the key word or idea and the children providing the description or explanation; the children invent their own bingo cards)
	– Dominoes (e.g. dominoes can be designed that require matching of ideas and explanations; the children work in pairs; domino sets can be designed to work with individual science topics; children can design their own dominoes)
	– Question dice (e.g. a dice can be made from a cube of wood on to which the question starters are written: 'Why ...?', 'What if ...?', 'How could you have ...?', 'What would ...?', 'If ... then ...?'. Leave one side blank with just a large question mark for the children to invent their own question. For a given topic, the child rolls the dice and asks a question that uses the starter. The child's partner has to answer it and then takes a turn rolling the dice and asking a question. The process can be modelled by the teacher beforehand. Alternatively, the children could make a paper dice for themselves using a cube net and write their own creative questions)
Plenaries/other ideas	These are useful in plenary sessions, to end a session in a fun way, or to generate discussion about contemporary issues:
	– What if ...? games (e.g. What if there was no electricity?; What if the ice caps melt completely?)
	– Ideas balls (e.g. made from white plastic footballs, each one marked using the tessellating shapes as ideas patches using a permanent marker to mark out the tessellations and write key words in each shape [e.g. for the electricity ball, it could have circuit, battery, parallel, series, buzzer, ...]; the children stand in a circle and the teacher throws the ball to a child. He/she catches it and whichever word his/her left thumb is resting on, that is the word to be explained)

Scientific creativity in investigative activities

Science is a process, a way of thinking and working. In the National Curriculum in England, this is the programme of study known as Science 1: Scientific Enquiry. But we cannot 'enquire' in a vacuum – we have to enquire about something, in this case the areas of science (in essence, astronomy, biology, chemistry, geology and physics). One aspect of this enquiry is the use of practical work to explore and investigate the ideas underpinning these areas of science. The use of practical work to enhance creativity is discussed by Haigh (2003) in the context of New Zealand biology classrooms. She criticizes the tendency for teachers to provide recipe-following practical work and recommends more open-ended investigations that provide opportunity for possibility thinking (see Craft 2000).

A similar call for open-ended investigations is made by Roberts (2009) who talks about pupils using them to work creatively to solve a problem. She cites examples of problems and argues that such creative uses of science share the common feature of not being available in a 'ready-to-use recipe format' in textbooks, relying instead on transfer of ideas to new situations. She provides an account of how such open-ended investigations would work. In the problem-solving situation, pupils have to work through a series of steps or stages:

- engage actively with substantive ideas from science;
- select and transfer them to aid the decisions required;
- make individual decisions based on an understanding of the ideas of science; and
- respond to the situations as they make their way through the problem to make their claim.

Note the appearance of decision making, which is characteristic of creative activity (Sternberg 2006).

Scientific creativity in problem solving

In the USA, Maker *et al.* (2008) encourage creativity through a project called DESCRIBE (Discovering Intellectual Strengths and Capabilities while Observing Varied Ethnic Responses). The team created a curriculum model which required problem solving for use with elementary school children and which could underpin the development of intelligence (or more specifically, giftedness) and creativity. They provide examples of problems from the programme that reflect varying degrees of structure. From their observation of classrooms while the pupils were doing activities designed to promote problem solving and creative thinking, they noted a number of characteristics of the lessons that might encourage creative and productive thinking and problems solving:

- the experience involved freedom of choice;
- the pupils set their own goals and decided how to meet them;
- there was open discussion of possibilities;

- a challenge was provided (to create something);
- pupils had the opportunity to work independently or collaboratively;
- probing questions from the teacher encouraged explanation and justification;
- pupils helped to define clear expectations of what the product needs to do; and
- a presentation of the products was made in which pupils interact with each other.

All of these goals can be met through open-ended problem solving.

Technology is probably one of the most obvious vehicles for this, fitting well with the third field for creative thought in science discussed earlier. Design and technology is sometimes described as the 'appliance of science' and, through its problem-focused approach, provides opportunities for the practical applications of skills that encourage creative thought. Davies (2009: 168) states that, 'In order to "create", pupils need confidence to learn in areas that are unfamiliar'. She suggests that designing and making activities enable pupils to reflect on their own thinking process and clarify and reflect upon their problem-solving strategies. Teachers can enable pupils to be creative by providing lessons in which children have the time to use different strategies to generate a wide range of design ideas, drawing on skills, knowledge and understanding to make their chosen solution.

Summary

As far as science and technology are concerned, what can teachers do to encourage creative thought and problem solving? To encourage creativity, the primary science classroom needs to be one in which:

- understanding is valued more than memory;
- all children are expected to contribute ideas;
- contributions are valued and respected;
- involvement is supported to meet different needs; and
- projects and challenges are targeted.

Within this context the teacher takes on different roles. At different times and for different purposes he or she acts as a resources provider, a guide, a facilitator, a hint provider or a change agent. By doing so, he or she ensures there is variety in the experiences offered by providing rich and varied opportunities for scientifically creative thought in the three fields described earlier. The relevance of the experiences is made explicit so pupils know why they are doing things and how the science fits into their lives. An appropriate classroom environment in which there is a positive ethos that supports question asking and answering, possibility thinking and risk taking, is established. The teacher guides the direction and development of creative thought through various scaffolding strategies and learns to recognize and evaluate both the creative process and its product.

All children may benefit from this but those who are particularly scientifically gifted are likely to be ready for independent, productive thought quite early. To provide it almost on a routine basis calls for a teacher who not only knows what scientific creativity means but is also confident in his or her own understandings of scientific ideas and processes.

References

Aguirre, J.M., Haggerty, S.M. and Linder, C.J. (1990) 'Student-teachers' conceptions of science, teaching and learning: a case study in pre-service science education', *International Journal of Science Education*, 12(4): 381–90.

Amabile, T. (2002) 'Creativity under the gun', *Harvard Business Review*, 80(8): 52–61.

Beetlestone, F. (1998) *Creative Children, Imaginative Teaching*, Buckingham: Open University Press.

Bell, R.L., Lederman, N.G. and Abd-El-Khalick, F. (2000) 'Developing and acting upon one's conception of the nature of science: a follow up study', *Journal of Research in Science Teaching*, 37(6): 563–81.

Beswick, K. (2004) 'The impact of teachers' perceptions of student characteristics on the enactment of their beliefs', *Proceedings of the 28th Conference of the International Group for the Psychology of Mathematics Education (IGPME), Vol. 2, Bergen*, (pp. 111–8), Cape Town, IGPME. Also Online. Available at http://www.emis.ams.org/proceedings/PME28/ (accessed 24 October 2010).

Bore, A. (2006) 'Bottom-up for creativity in science?: a collaborative model for curriculum and professional development', *Journal of Education for Teaching*, 32(4): 413–22.

Braund, M. and Driver, R. (2005) 'Pupils' perceptions of practical science in primary and secondary school: implications for improving progression and continuity of learning', *Educational Research*, 4(1): 77–91.

Brickhouse, N. and Bodner, G.M. (1992) 'The beginning science teacher: classroom narratives of conviction and constraints', *Journal of Research in Science Teaching*, 29(5): 471–85.

Craft, A. (2000) *Creativity Across the Primary Curriculum: Framing and developing practice*, London: Routledge.

Craft, A. (2002) *Creativity and Early Years Education*, London: Continuum.

Davies, D., Howe, A., Rogers, M. and Fasciato, M. (2004) 'How do trainee primary teachers understand creativity?', in E. Norman, D. Spendlove, P. Graver and A. Mitchell (eds) *Creativity and Innovation – DATA International Research Conference*, Wellesbourne: Design and Technology Association. Online. Project website available at http://www.bathspa.ac.uk/schools/education/projects/creative-teachers/default.asp (accessed 20 March 2010).

Davies, L. (2009) 'Design and technology's contribution to the development of the use of language, numeracy, ICT, key skills, creativity and innovation and thinking skills', *Journal of Design and Technology Education*, 5(2): 166–70.

Dickinson, V.L., Abd-El-Khalick, F.S. and Lederman, N.G. (2000) *Changing Elementary Teachers' Views of the NOS: effective strategies for science method courses*, ERIC No: ED 441 680.

Duschl, R.A. and Wright, E. (1989) 'A case study of high school teachers' decision-making models for planning and teaching science', *Journal of Research in Science Teaching*, 26(6): 467–501.

Fryer, M. and Collings, J.A. (1991) 'Teachers' views about creativity', *British Journal of Educational Psychology*, 61: 207–19.

Hadamard, J. (1954) *The Psychology of Invention in the Mathematical Field*, New York: Dover Publications.

Haigh, M. (2003) 'Enhancing creativity through investigative practical work in science'. Paper presented at the *New Zealand Association of Research in Education* Conference, *Auckland*, 29 November–3 December.

Hoang, T. (2007) 'Creativity: a motivational tool for interest and conceptual understanding in science education', *International Journal of Human and Social Sciences*, 1(4): 215–21.

Hofer, B.K. and Pintrich, P.R. (1997) 'The development of epistemological theories: beliefs about knowledge and knowing and their relation to learning', *Review of Educational Research*, 67: 88–140.

Jeffrey, B. and Craft, A. (2001) 'Introduction: the universalization of creativity', in A. Craft, A., B. Jeffrey and M. Leibling (eds) *Creativity in Education*, London: Continuum.

Kind, P.M. and Kind, V. (2007) 'Creativity in science education: perspectives and challenges for developing school science', *Studies in Science Education*, 43: 1–37.

Klahr, D. and Dunbar, K. (1998) 'Dual space search during scientific reasoning', *Cognitive Science*, 12: 1–48.

Lunn, S. (2002) 'What we think we can safely say …: primary teachers' views of the nature of science', *British Educational Research Journal*, 28(5): 649–72.

Maker, C.J., Jo, S. and Muammar, O.M. (2008) 'Development of creativity: The influence of varying levels of implementation of the DISCOVER curriculum model, a non-traditional pedagogical approach', *Learning and Individual Differences*, 18: 402–17.

Maloney, J., Keogh, B., Naylor, S., Downing, B. and Simon, S. (n.d.) 'Using puppets in the classroom to get children talking about their ideas', Online. Available at http:// www.puppetsproject.com/documents/puppets-t-earth-sci06.doc (accessed 20 March 2010).

Mellado, V. (1997) 'Preservice teachers' classroom practice and their conceptions of the nature of science', *Science and Education*, 6(4): 331–54.

Newton, D.P. (1989) *Making Science Education Relevant*, London: Kogan Page.

Newton, D.P. (2008) *Talking Sense in Science*, London: Routledge.

Newton, D.P. and Newton, L.D. (2009a) 'A procedure for assessing textbook support for reasoned thinking', *Asia-Pacific Education Researcher*, 18(1), 109–16.

Newton, D.P. and Newton, L.D. (2009b) 'Some student teachers' conceptions of creativity in school science', *Research in Science and Technological Education*, 27(1): 45–60.

Newton, L.D. (1997) 'Teachers' questioning for understanding in science', *British Journal of Curriculum and Assessment*, 8: 28–32.

Newton, L.D. and Newton, D.P. (2010a) 'What teachers see as creative incidents in elementary science lessons', *International Journal of Science Education*, 32(15), 1989–2005.

Newton, L.D. and Newton, D.P. (2010b) 'Creative thinking and teaching for creativity in elementary school science', *Gifted and Talented International*, 25(3): 111–23.

Osborne, J., Collins, S., Ratcliffe, M., Millar, R. and Duschl, R. (2001) 'What 'ideas-about-science' should be taught in school science? A Delphi Study of the Expert Community', Paper presented at the *Sixth History, Philosophy and Science Teaching Conference, Denver, Colorado*, November 7–11.

Pajares, M.F. (1992) 'Teachers' beliefs and educational research: cleaning up a messy construct', *Review of Educational Research*, 62: 307–32.

Qualifications and Curriculum Authority (QCA) (2008) *The Aims of the Curriculum*. Online. Available at http://curriculum.qca.org.uk/uploads/Aims_of_the_curriculum_tcm8-1812.pdf?return=/key-stages-3-and-4/aims/index.aspx (accessed November 2010).

Roberts, R. (2009) 'Can teaching about evidence encourage a creative approach in open-ended investigations?' *School Science Review*, 90(332): 31–8.

Scottish Executive Education Department (SEED) (2006) 'Promoting creativity in education: overview of key national policy developments across the UK', Online. Available at http://www.hmie.gov.uk/documents/publications/hmiepcie.html (accessed October 2010).

Sternberg, R.J. (2006) 'The nature of creativity', *Creativity Research Journal*, 18(1): 87–98.

Strauss, S. (1993) 'Teachers' pedagogical content knowledge about children's minds and learning: implications for teacher education', *Educational Psychologist*, 28: 279–90.

Waters-Adams, S. (2006) 'The relationship between understanding the nature of science and practice: the influence of teachers' beliefs about education, teaching and learning', *International Journal of Science Education*, 28(8): 919–44.

5

Creativity in Art and Music

Douglas Newton, Hazel Donkin, Dimitra Kokotsaki and Lynn Newton

Introduction

Traditionally, when people think of creative experience in school, they think of 'the Arts'. Consequently, teaching for creativity in subjects like art and music might seem to be non-problematic. If, as the various research studies indicate, teachers generally see these two subjects as offering great potential for creative activity, then these should be straightforward areas. But are they? Art, drama, dance and music, for instance, do indeed offer opportunities for imagination, self-expression, exploring possibilities and generally 'doing it your own way' (Eisner 1965). But there is more to it than this. While self-expression may bring novelty to the activity, we have to remember that this expression also has to be in some way successful, seen to have value or otherwise have some 'rightness of fit' (Csikszentmihalyi 1996; Siegemund 1998). And, of course, it is generally considered better if it does this in some aesthetically satisfying way. Even this is not all of it; creativity is not just in what the artist, writer or composer does but is also in what those who make something of their work do. Here, we exemplify the so-called creative arts with the school subjects of art and music.

Creativity in art and music

Art education can be justified in various ways and the experience of creativity it offers is one of them (Lanier 1975; Fleming 2010). Sharp and Le Métais (2000) studied 19 countries' aims of art education and found that artistic creativity is widely valued. United Nations Educational, Scientific and Cultural Organization (UNESCO) (2006) has argued that art offers an opportunity to develop creative potential and imagination, thereby empowering people and enabling them to take part in cultural and artistic activities (Eisner 1965, 2002; Lanier 1975; Shillito *et al.* 2008). Exploring possibilities, exercising imagination and self-expression and resisting cultural homogeneity may also foster some kinds of democratic behaviour (Siegemund 1998).

Nevertheless, for many years, artists were seen as artisans or craftsmen who replicated and captured a physical likeness. Although now commonly seen as the archetype of creative activities, the nature of artistic creativity is still the subject of debate (Prentice 2000; Claxton *et al.* 2006). One problem is that there are many varieties and ways of working in art and it is difficult to distil their creative essence into a concise statement. Even artists have difficulty defining artistic creativity: when asked what it is, Picasso said he did not know and, even if he did, he would not say (Swanger 1990). The general view, however, is that seeing artistic creativity as something mystical and inexplicable is not appropriate (Osborne 2003). Wright (1990) describes it as a learned and practised activity with a purposeful, expressive end. The problem facing artists is how to achieve that end. It is in the 'how' that the creativity lies. Imagination is needed to envisage what the end might be and to construct a way of getting there (Dineen and Collins 2005) and it involves the deliberate manipulation and integration of materials so that they capture what is to be expressed (Eisner 1993; Seefeldt 1995; Wolcott 1996). This process may be neither easy nor entirely conscious (Gaut and Livingston 2003; Claxton 2006) but that is where artistic creativity lies. Novelty may, indeed, be reflected in the product – as in Brunelleschi's use of scientific perspective in the Italian Renaissance and Monet's capture of light in nineteenth-century Impressionism – but it lies in the process of production. This is important as it means that an artistic product could appear to be relatively commonplace (e.g. another portrait, albeit skilfully executed and well-crafted) yet still have demanded creative effort in its making (Sennett 2008). As Sternberg (2006) has pointed out, creativity involves choice and decisions. Imagination is what provides the choice and in taking a decision, the artist is being creative.

Of course, creativity is not confined to the artist or the composer. The viewer of a picture is not a passive onlooker or receiver of the artist's 'message' but responds to the picture in a more or less personal way and constructs something of personal significance from it (Hirsch 1967; Thomas 1991). In other words, creativity does not end with the finishing of the product but begins again with each new viewer. Similarly, in music, it does not end with a composition. The composition is interpreted by the person who plays it and the listener who responds to it in turn. The composer, player and the listener are each more or less creative in their interaction with the work.

Explicit attention may need to be given to notions of creativity in all subjects, including art and music. The danger is that, because these are seen as archetypal creative activities, it is assumed that everyone knows what it means to be creative in art and in music or in the other arts, for that matter.

Conceptions of artistic creativity

Studies in the USA found non-artists saw creativity as evident in a product's novel, unusual nature stemming from the artist's personal, original approach. Art teachers felt that creativity lay in a work's novelty, unusual combination and composition (Beattie 2000; Stricker 2008). Creativity may be seen as an exceptional talent – you either have it or you don't (Osborne 2003). Whatever talent you have, however, these teachers saw it as potentially open to development through instruction, experience and practice (Craft 2002; Stricker 2008). In Austria, a study of artists found them to believe that creative people are imaginative, talented, unconventional, intellectual, hard working and risk takers (Glück *et al.* 2002). A study of final-year history of art students in the UK (Newton and Donkin 2011) found them generally to associate art with opportunities for freedom, originality and imagination which at least some saw as potentially being in the process. They generally saw artistic creativity as being directed towards a specific end and they valued originality and craftsmanship as means to that end. This creativity, however, could be seen as something artists are born with, although the gift could be nurtured or trained. Such views were similar to those of artists and art teachers elsewhere. However, generalities can conceal misconceptions and diverse notions of artistic creativity. For instance, some could not see that viewers are creative in constructing a personal meaning of a work of art; others did not show an awareness of the relevance of rightness of fit and some seemed to reserve the term 'originality' for major stylistic innovation. In short, these students' beliefs about artistic creativity were quite varied (Newton and Donkin 2011).

Students like these, and others with less experience of art, commonly seek teaching careers in the primary school. Those with broad, inclusive views of artistic creativity could be well suited to fostering creativity in the art classroom. Those with narrow views, however, are likely to encourage and favour only what they see as matters. For instance, rightness of fit and the decisions which produce it may be seen as irrelevant.

Fostering creativity and problem solving in art

Although the concern here is with fostering creative activity, this does not mean that opportunities to learn the capabilities of the materials and practise in using them are unwelcome. Nor does it mean that the 'happy accident' which produces something novel is unwelcome if that accident is recognized as improving the rightness of fit. But, sooner or later, we have to provide opportunities for purposeful creativity. However, not just anything goes: there must be some possibility-thinking and decision-making, conscious or otherwise, which leads to some rightness of fit of the product (Siegemund 1998; Sternberg 2006). The child's efforts are directed towards a particular end, not just any end. So, for instance, if the end is a birthday card then a gloomy card, however imaginative, would not normally be appropriate. Table 5.1 offers some suggestions as starting points which can be adapted for children of different ages, experiences and abilities. At the same time, we must not forget that the child can also be a viewer and appraiser of art. This is not a passive activity but calls for a creative engagement with a product in which the child constructs a personal response to or an interpretation of it. Table 5.1 concludes with some illustrative activities for children to engage with products in this way.

Conceptions of music creativity

While promoting creativity in education is recognized as important [consider, for instance, its central role within the new music National Curriculum: Qualifications and Curriculum Development Agency (QCDA) 2007], relatively little research has been conducted on creative processes in music (Hallam 2006). In recent years, the perception

TABLE 5.1 Starting points for creative thinking through art

MEDIUM/FOCUS	ACTIVITY
Making images/ pictures	– Produce a picture/image that will tell a visitor what kind of person you are.
	– Produce a picture to show what you think you will look like when you grow up/what kind of person you will be.
	– Design an advertisement or poster to attract people to buy a …
	– Design a poster to attract people to the school play/pantomime.
	– Design a picture of a clown to cheer up a sick friend.
	– Make a picture to show me what 'a riot of colour'/'rough diamond'/'seeing red'/'feeling light hearted'/'in a dark mood'/'green with envy'/'blue with cold' mean.
	– King Kong takes over the country. Make a new postage stamp to celebrate the event.
Making images/ symbols	– Create a bookplate for your friend's books that reflects what interests him/her.
	– Design a gift tag for a special birthday gift.
	– Create a new road sign to warn people about using mobile phones when driving.
	– Create a 'good feeling' map for children who are new to your school.
	– Create new symbols for a weather map.
	– Create a banner or placard for an eco-warrior.
Working with clay	– Produce a door plaque that tells us something about the kind of people who live in the house (e.g. friendly, untidy, busy, …).
	– Create an object out of clay that tells a visitor something about what you like/dislike/how you feel.
	– Create an ornament for grandparents' garden or windowsill.
	– Create a commemorative object for someone famous or for an important event.
	– Make a gargoyle for the teacher's desk to scare away naughty children.
Working with patterns	– Use vegetable printing to create a new wallpaper for your bedroom.
	– Use marbling to create borders on writing paper to make a Happy Birthday gift.
Working with fabrics	– Make a gift for someone using fabrics, yarns, etc.
	– Santa has had enough of wearing a red outfit every year. Design a new one for him. Use fabrics to show the outfit as a collage picture.
	– Design and make a collage picture to show a new school uniform.
	– Use fabrics, threads and yarns to make a picture to represent a season.

MEDIUM/FOCUS	ACTIVITY
	– Weave a table mat which shows what you think about some food you dislike a lot.
Working with other materials	– Find a new, decorative use for [shells, seeds, …] – the children are allowed to use an appropriate range of art and design materials and tools.
	– Use recycled materials to make the scariest scarecrow.
	– You have seen a corn dolly. I want you to make a corn animal.
	– Create a stained glass window (using coloured tissue paper) for a special celebration or building.
	– Create a mosaic floor design for a kitchen using coloured paper.
	– Collect rubbings of different textured surfaces and make a moonscape picture using these rubbings.
Creating meaning from art	– Turn a set of shapes into an object or picture – ask a friend to identify what it is. Ask him or her to do the same for you.
	– Use paint to create 'paint blot tests' and test friends to see what they 'see' in your blot. What do their blots look like to you?
	– Ask children to look at famous paintings (or other works of art) and tell the story:
	■ What is the person in the picture thinking/feeling?
	■ Why do you think that?
	■ What are the people doing? Why?
	■ What time of year is it? Why do you think this?
	■ What happens next?
	■ How has the artist made the person look happy/sad/ … angry/ frightened/brave, etc.?
	■ Why has the artist made that person feel that way?
	■ How does the picture make you feel?
	■ What is it about the picture which makes you feel like that?
	■ What do you think the artist is trying to show you in the picture?
	■ How did the artist do it?

of creativity as being achievable only by a limited number of talented people has shifted towards a more democratic definition in which everyone can be creative in some area, given the right conditions and support [National Advisory Committee on Creative and Cultural Education (NACCCE) 1999]. Musical creativity, in general, and more specifically improvisation as a certain form of creative behaviour, has been defined as a learnable and teachable high-level skill (Balkin 1990) that can develop with learning, practice and experience (Koutsoupidou and Hargreaves 2009).

The creative process can generally be described as the thinking that takes place as a person is planning to construct a creative product. This is defined as an active, constructed and dynamic mental process which swings between convergent (factual) and divergent (imaginative) thinking (Webster 1990, 2002) with creativity closely related to the latter. Divergent thinking, in particular, includes qualities such as *musical extensiveness* (the number of ideas generated through open-ended questions) and *flexibility* and *originality* (Swanwick and Tillman 1986). A significant component of creative growth is the development of the decision-making process which helps connections to be made 'where connections were not previously apparent' – the heart of creativity is about 'connections, connections, and connections' (Balkin 1990: 30). In the primary music classroom, creativity is about musical imagination, pupils' ability to 'hear' and create the music in their heads [Office for Standards in Education (Ofsted) 2009].

Musical creativity can be demonstrated through composition and improvisation, regarded as the main activities for generating new ideas in music. However, in more recent research, music listening and performance have been considered as additional forms of creative behaviour (Reimer 1989; Dunn 1997; Koutsoupidou and Hargreaves 2009). Balkin (1990) and Kratus (1990) have defined creativity in music by focusing on its components, what they call the three Ps of the creativity equation, the person, the process and the product (Balkin 1990). This helps educationalists generate specific goals and objectives for creative learning. Jeffrey and Woods (2009) added a physical component of *place* as the fourth P, the place where creative learning is situated and which can promote a sense of ownership and belonging.

Kratus (1990) believes that a creative person can show traits such as *originality* (producing unusual or uncommon responses), *fluency* (producing a number of responses to a problem) and *flexibility* (producing responses that are different from each other). These enable engagement in the activities of composing, improvising and performing music. Fluency, flexibility and originality are three of the four scales (the fourth one being *elaboration*, the amount of detail in responses) that form part of the Torrance Tests of Creative Thinking as they were first developed in 1966 (in Kyung 2006). These personal qualities echo Webster's (1990) enabling skills which include *musical aptitudes, conceptual understanding, craftsmanship* and *aesthetic sensitivity*, in short, any personal characteristics, musical background and knowledge that facilitate the creative process.

The creative process starts with an idea or intention and finishes with a creative product. The four stages of Wallas's (1926) creative thinking – *preparation, incubation, illumination* and *verification* – have often been used to talk about engagement in the creative process and show how an initial idea or intention can develop and lead to a creative product. The creative process becomes functional, however, within an enabling, 'scaffolding' environment (Sawyer 2006), where the teacher, for instance, might set up initial boundaries and provide certain material for pupils to use during the creative activity (Wilson 2001), or decide that a balanced interdependence of constraints and freedom (Burnard and Younker 2002) might work better in some cases in helping pupils think more imaginatively and make the most appropriate aesthetic choices. According to Kratus (1990), exploration, improvisation, composition and creative performance are the four types of music activity that pupils are expected to engage in as part of the creative process.

Finally, musical products could be analysed on the basis of how musical elements or musical principles such as repetition, development and contrast, are used in original ways (Kratus 1990). A key element of the creative product is that it cannot be predetermined by the teacher and, therefore, its exact nature can be largely unpredictable. This seems to contribute to the difficulty in assessing originality when referring to pupils' music making

(NACCCE 1999). A vital stage, however, after the completion of the musical product is the evaluation or reflection phase where the musical product is verified and assessed by both the teacher and the pupil who created the piece of work. The aim is that, by reflecting on and evaluating the strengths and weaknesses of the musical product against the initial objectives, pupils can move to the next cycle of creating music with renewed knowledge and understanding, and make effective musical progress as a result. Balkin (1990: 32) has emphasized this talking about the 're-' factor by suggesting that when anyone is being creative they 'must continually rethink, reconsider, replace, refine, redo, reaffirm, reprocess, rewrite, and reconceptualize'.

Conceptions of creativity in music

The meaning ascribed to creativity by classroom teachers is vital in its effective implementation, as the way creativity is encouraged will be highly dependent on teachers' ability to recognize, understand and support pupils' creativity (Cropley 2001). In music, some recent studies have attempted to address the scarcity of research on what creativity means and how it might be perceived by music teachers (Odena 2001; Crow 2008; Zbainos and Anastasopoulou 2008; Odena and Welch 2009; Kokotsaki 2011).

The value of creativity

Creative behaviour seems to be correlated with a sense of satisfaction in individual and group work (MacDonald *et al.* 2006). Csikszentmihalyi (1998) maintains creativity brings about an inner experience of fulfilment, not only in intellectual, emotional and physical terms, but also as far as the quality of communication with other people is concerned. These positive feelings are associated with the link between creativity and people's mastery over their environment, their ability to make choices and implement these in their lives resulting in an enhanced sense of self and social identity (Craft 2000). In particular, according to Ansdell (1995: 104), 'in contrast to being limited, dull and stuck, the experience of being creative involves a motivation and an energy (that we sometimes call inspiration)'.

Moreover, the creativity of an idea or product is not evaluated by reference to its own qualities, but in terms of the effect it is able to produce in others who are exposed to it and is a phenomenon that emerges through an interaction between producer and audience (Csikszentmihalyi 1998). For instance, Moore (1990) urges educators to encourage their pupils to spend more time and effort in creating musical products that would be satisfying to other listeners, as the perception of an audience can make 'fragmented experiments' develop into 'successful compositions'.

The prevalence of music in children's lives and the role of creativity

Music is a vital part of children's everyday lives. The 3½-year-old children in Lamont's study (2008) were actively involved in music making and experienced approximately twice the amount of music through a variety of different media as adults do in their waking hours. Children grow with and through music, as they make it themselves or are immersed in the sounds that surround them, in a way that feeds their identity. According to Campbell (2000), the personal, social and emotional impact of music is vast. Campbell maintains that it is a teacher's responsibility to prepare authentic programmes of school music based on children's real needs and interests and that getting a close glimpse of children's musical realities can help teachers develop more effective teaching strategies for children's emotional and mental development. Expert guidance and formal learning rooted in children's informal learning experiences is important to fully enrich and give meaning to their lives. This holds particular importance for the earliest years of formal education, where experiences that stimulate children's interest in music (Ellison and Creech 2010) and encourage their creativity (Hallam and Rogers 2010) can be very beneficial. The development of musical creativity, in particular, can reinforce listening and musical understanding, and enhance personal and social development in addition to developing creative skills more generally (Hallam and Rogers 2010).

The role of the primary teacher

Schools can play a major role in helping children develop a positive musical identity by encouraging active participation in musical activities. This is considered important for positive identification with school music lessons and with school in general (Lamont 2001). In addition, active engagement with music positively affects creativity (see Hallam 2010). Even though not all musical activities require creativity, the desire and motivation to explore different sounds and develop a new idea should permeate the whole process of building up musical skills through practice and study (Hennessy 2009). In other words, teachers should aim to instil in pupils a creative attitude to all music making through the development of imagination and activities that encourage meaningful exploration of sound.

Teachers' conceptions of creativity in music

Odena and Welch (2009) developed a generative model of teachers' thinking on musical creativity, arguing that teachers' perceptions of musical creativity are influenced by their prior in- and out-of-school experiences and can be modified through their constant interaction within the teaching environment. Much of the work into teachers conceptions, however, has been at the secondary school level (Crow 2008; Zbainos and Anastasopoulou 2008; Russell-Bowie 2009; Kokotsaki 2011).

Student teachers in primary education talk highly about the value of creative musical activities for primary age pupils as they recognize a wide range of benefits (Kokotsaki in press). The benefits identified for pupils when they start thinking creatively in music included the transferability of the skill in other subject areas, building up confidence and self-esteem, promoting a 'can do' attitude and encouraging, therefore, a kind of independent thinking that can replace feelings of worry about a particular problem or task with a willingness to try out and explore. For these student teachers, a creative lesson was associated with more interest by the pupils, inspiration, lessons of better quality, enthusiasm and enjoyment, and also with musical understanding as pupils are given a chance to apply their knowledge and address any misconceptions.

Generally, all could articulate to some degree their views about what counts as creativity in the primary music classroom. For all, creativity in music was about making up sounds relevant to the task set. They understood that activities that involve creative musical thinking are those where children make their own choices or decisions, add something to or adapt a given idea. They recognized it as not about copying, reproducing a piece of music without contributing anything personal to it or about everyone doing the same thing as directed by the teacher. Most considered composing as offering the best chance for creative thought in music followed by performing, improvising, singing and listening. Singing or performing, for instance, can become creative activities if pupils can manipulate the musical elements, add variety to or change a song, or compose lyrics to go with a given tune. The most important component of creativity, according to these student teachers, is being given the freedom to interpret and create music how they choose. In other words, the pupils are required to use their imaginations, create mental representations of sounds by imagining them in their heads and then, through a thinking process of exploring options and using initiative, express themselves and come up with individual and often unique and original responses.

Not all student teachers conceptualized the creative process in the same way, but all mentioned some of these components. It was interesting that even though some who had had some musical training in the past felt more confident about their ability to teach music, about half of them did not feel that their ability to play an instrument would be sufficient to appropriately support pupils' creative music making in the primary classroom, particularly because they felt that they lacked enough relevant training themselves to be able to model the creative activities well enough for their pupils.

Some of the participants commented upon the limited time devoted to music in primary schools because of the standards culture where literacy and numeracy often take precedence over subjects such as music which are often considered of lesser importance. Some also mentioned that music was not promoted enough in their placement schools and, therefore, that its place on the timetable was limited. A small number of participants disappointingly reported examples of bad teaching in music.

Some problems associated with teaching music in the primary school

The teaching of classroom music by the generalist teacher has been described as patchy and unsatisfactory (Russell-Bowie 1993) with teachers often reporting feelings of inadequacy. Many generalists can be discouraged by composition and musical notation and often feel that they are not meeting the National Curriculum requirements for music (Holden and Button 2006) or may struggle to incorporate creativity in their schemes of work (Hallam *et al.* 2009b).

Related to these feelings of inadequacy is the well-documented low teacher confidence in music compared to other subjects (Holden and Button 2006; Hallam *et al.* 2009a, 2009b). This contributes to perceptions of music being one of the most difficult foundation subjects to cover at Key Stages 1 and 2 [Qualifications and Curriculum Authority (QCA) 2005]. This negative attitude to teaching music is often exacerbated by it having little time in the curriculum, by limited or no access to music experiences on teaching practice (Hennessy 2000) or by music teaching being covered by teaching assistants or visiting specialist teachers to give planning, preparation and assessment (PPA) time to classroom teachers (Hallam *et al.* 2009b). This was evident from the comments of the student teachers, discussed earlier. There is, however, what Ellison and Creech (2010) call a 'discordance' between what happens in practice and the emphasis on the value of music education underpinning the government's primary strategy [Department for Children, Schools and Families (DCSF) 2003] and recent reviews of the primary curriculum (e.g. Rose 2009).

Russell-Bowie (2009) investigated the perceptions of teachers in elementary schools in five countries about the priorities and challenges of music teaching and found it was a low priority. They felt challenged by a lack of resources, time, subject knowledge, preparation time and personal musical experience. Hennessy (2006) highlights the importance of having someone who can lead to music provision on the permanent school staff, making it meaningful, demanding, fun and engaging for all children and offering good access to enrichment activities for teachers. Ellison and Creech (2010: 224) also stress that strong subject leadership is crucial to helping raise standards in music provision and give young pupils the chance 'to achieve their potential in relation to musical skills, transferable skills and creativity'. As Craft (2002) argues, creativity is not a knowledge-free skill. In order for an individual to operate creatively in any knowledge domain, they must have developed an understanding of that domain. That understanding must first be acquired by the teacher before there is any chance for primary age pupils to think creatively in music.

Fostering creative thinking and problem solving in music

Creativity and music are so closely interlinked that any aspect of music teaching and learning should have creativity as its heart. There is often the perception that certain musical activities are more creative than others, like composition and improvisation, where the child needs to create something new and personal. However, it is important to highlight that even activities that require the development of knowledge and instrumental skill, which are often perceived to be more mechanical and requiring copying and repetition, should be driven by creative impulse, by the desire to use musical imagination, understand the musical purpose of skill development and exercise one's understanding, skills and musical judgement to make decisions and communicate the music with personal expressiveness and meaning.

The role of the teacher in recognizing children's creative abilities and fostering the conditions where these can be realized is crucial. The most important enablers of creativity in the music classroom are the teacher's strong belief in children's creative potential and overt recognition of their creative acts (Barnes 2009), and a supportive climate where 'short, frequent, supported, invited experiences' can encourage ownership and help build confidence and competence (Jones and Robson 2008).

An interesting way to describe the context for creative behaviour is the idea of 'getting messy with the elements of music' (Bunting 2011). This implies an engagement with all musical activities through the integration of composing, improvising, performing, listening and responding. Active and attentive listening is essential, linking the musical product with the way it is imagined and intended and encouraging its constant improvement and refinement. Music technology offers a range of opportunities for creative musical activities by helping children build a repertoire of ideas over time.

The creative act has been conceptualized as a four-stage process with a number of theorists revisiting Wallas' initial theory (1926) and further describing and exemplifying each of the four stages (e.g. Ross 1980; Casson 2011). Table 5.2 describes these four stages of the creative process in the context of music teaching and learning.

Stage 1: the identification of the idea or intention

The goal is the emergence of the creative idea when the teacher provides pupils with a stimulus or a framework that can be used as a starting point. The teacher provides the initial building blocks, the tools that pupils can use to create. A balance needs to be struck here between providing a rigid, set structure while allowing room for flexibility and development of own ideas. Ideas for creative work might include:

- pieces of music and events (making own tribal ceremony);
- writing a story and composing the music for a film plot;
- writing a pop song and thinking about its structure and lyrics;
- creating a ring tone for a mobile phone;
- making a soundscape composition around a story;
- using graphic scores to depict the music;
- making instruments while exploring their different pitches;
- creating and putting together sequences of sounds;
- embracing other art forms and composing music in response to a painting;
- finding musical ideas in poetry or dance, or;
- writing music to depict different characters and their actions in a story.

There are ample opportunities for creative work and creative expression in performing and singing when children are encouraged to create their own interpretation and make decisions about how to arrange the piece or sing the song.

Stage 2: playing with ideas and considering possibilities

Having developed or been given an initial idea, the pupils start *experimenting* and *exploring* different options, different ways of using the instruments in order to realize ideas and create a musical product. These processes of experimenting and exploring are not simple; they require an ability to think outside the box and express oneself in order to generate creative ways of reaching the goal.

Being able to use *imagination* and identify emotions, feelings, thoughts and ideas and *self-expression* assists the experimentation process. A range of options become available as individuals are encouraged to identify and use personal preferences through the expression of thoughts and feelings.

TABLE 5.2 The four stages of the creative process in music

	STAGE 1	STAGE 2	STAGE 3	STAGE 4
What is it?	Identification of the idea or intention	Playing with the idea; thinking about it, considering possibilities	Refining ideas and developing the necessary skills	Structuring, presenting and evaluating the result
The four stages exemplified – main focus	Creative idea using a stimulus/structure – Ideas might include: 　■ pieces of music 　■ events 　■ stories 　■ films 　■ using graphic scores 　■ making own instruments 　■ sequences of sounds 　■ other art forms – 　　paintings, poetry, dance	Experimenting – Self-expression and using imagination – Key factors: 　■ teacher as skilful facilitator 　■ teacher modelling 　■ improvisation 　■ time and space	Thinking – an active and dynamic process – Key processes – Mental engagement and thoughtful planning is key during the creative process	Decision making – Personal creation that has originality and variety – Key processes – Group work – Reflection and evaluation – Communication of the creative product
Focus on the *quality* of the output through:	Composing, improvising, performing (singing and developing instrumental skills), listening, reviewing and appraising, using music technology			
Enabling environment and the role of the teacher	– Belief in and recognition of children's creative potential – Supportive climate to encourage ownership and build confidence and competence			

Facilitating the creative flow in the lesson is crucial at this stage. The teacher needs to be a skilful facilitator, intervening sensitively to encourage ideas to be tried and suggesting ways to combine them or give feedback to pupils' suggestions (Bunting 2011). The teacher can also help through musical prompts that model musical ideas to encourage flow and progress during the creative process. Teacher's modelling can allow the process of imitation to occur where 'ideas are remade, interpreted and perhaps transformed' by nurturing children's imagination (Jones and Robson 2008). It is at this stage of experimenting and considering possibilities that improvisation acquires a central role (Hallam and Rogers 2010). Children's improvised ideas can form the building blocks of their final musical composition. But they need time and space to allow their intentions to come into fruition and start combining these ideas into a concrete form (Jones and Robson 2008).

Stage 3: refining ideas and developing skills

Pupils who are engaged creatively in composition are able to demonstrate that they have developed deep thought processes while undertaking the task and they have devoted time and effort. Thinking is *an active and dynamic process* for them. They bring in different ideas which are the result of their mental engagement with the task. They have developed, therefore, the mental capacity to use thinking skills effectively in order to produce a creative piece of work. Pupils are dynamically engaged in exploring options, asking the teacher questions, refining their ideas, and developing the necessary skills in an attempt to create a clear picture of the outcome and then work towards reaching that goal. The ability to be involved in thoughtful planning in the process of creating a novel and coherent whole is considered to be the highest order thinking skill in Bloom's revised taxonomy of educational objectives (Krathwohl 2002).

Stage 4: structuring, presenting and evaluating the result

The final stage involves *decision making*. Pupils make small personal choices along the way. The creative piece of work is one that shows that the pupil has moved away from the teacher's ideas, from basic ideas that the teacher provided. Instead, they used these as examples to then be engaged in a dynamic process of exploring, thinking, discussing in groups and making decisions. This decision-making process signifies having control over the creative process/product, being involved in a constant process of making choices, evaluating and making adjustments to improve and make the composition sound better. Group work is of vital importance here as children work together, listen to each other, take risks, share ideas, make group choices, and evaluate and reflect on the result.

A significant attribute of the creative product is that it is personal and unique to the individual or the individual-as-part-of-the-group that created it. Their own creations have *originality and variety*: it 'comes from within'. It shows originality by the individual who produced, compared to previous work. It could also be the most original outcome when compared to the rest of the class work. This clearly illustrates the distinction between 'individual' and 'relative' originality as argued in the NACCCE report (1999: 32).

In addition to being unique to the individual and original, it needs to have variety, including a range of musical elements and techniques rather than being monotonous and, possibly, boring. It can also contain an element of unpredictability where the product deviates from the listener's expectation. This aspect of creativity in composing echoes a musical performance where the musical elements are elaborated to produce slight deviation from the written score that would go against the expectation of the listener. Finally, the creative product should not only exist in the mind of the creator but it also needs to be communicated and recognized as such. There seems to be an important difference here between having the potential for creativity and having the tools and confidence to express it. Reflection and evaluation of the creative product is a creative activity itself helping to instil in children understanding, a sense of ownership, and independence (Hennessy 2009).

The benefits of creative learning are many and varied. The development of creative skills can have both musical and extra-musical effects as children develop deeper learning and understanding by exercising their imagination and thinking skills, critical listening as well as the motivation to develop a more intimate relationship with music and a deeper insight into music making. When cross-curricular links with music are emphasized and interesting links with other areas of the curriculum are made, children's creative approach

TABLE 5.3 Ideas for creative activities in primary music

Early years (3–5)	– Producing a wide range of musical sounds and performing using homemade instruments or other materials, such as kitchen utensils, blocks and building textures
	– Encouraging children to talk about music and letting them express their emotional and imaginative responses
	– Noticing children's rhythmic movement play and guiding their movement into music
Primary school years (5–11)	– Composing music to accompany a story
	– Listening to music that represents distinct sounds (such as animal sounds or a train sound) and discussing what instruments or elements of the sounds create that effect
	– Making music to represent a particular sound theme, such as the weather
	– Dancing to a piece of music and explaining their rhythmic and expressive choices
	– Discussing the similarities and differences of music from different cultures and creating a piece of music using distinct sounds from a particular culture
Middle school years (9–13)	– Choosing a painting or sculpture and either individually, or in small groups, composing or improvising a piece of music in response
	– Exploring and imitating nature sounds using instruments
	– Writing a story for a fictional film and writing a short piece of music for each scene
	– Listening to a range of pop songs, picking out certain musical structures (e.g. riffs) and making up a new version of a pop song

towards music can enhance creative pursuits in other subject areas leading to an overall attitude of independent and original thinking. In addition, considering the rich musical experiences from outside school that all children to a greater or lesser extent are exposed to, cross-curricular links with music underline its important role in the social and cultural world in which children live and learn (Hennessy 2009). Some suggested starting points are provided in Table 5.3.

As Burnard (2009) argues, there is the danger that, as children grow older, their creative work can move away from personalized exploration and personal choices to modified forms of creative behaviour that are determined more by external factors such as curriculum, time and assessment constraints. In order not to jeopardize pupils' creative development in music, she encourages music educators to pay attention to the notion of progression in musical creativity building on earlier phases in line with children's musical and compositional maturation.

In conclusion

Explicit attention may need to be given to notions of creativity in all subjects, including art and music. The danger is that, because these are seen as archetypal creative activities, it is assumed that everyone knows what it means to be creative in art and in music or in the other arts, for that matter.

References

Ansdell, G. (1995) *Music for life: aspects of creative music therapy with adult clients*, London: Jessica Kingsley Publishers.

Balkin, A. (1990) 'What is creativity? What is it not?' *Music Educators Journal*, 76(9): 29–32.

Barnes, J. (2009) *Cross-curricular learning: 3–14*, London: Sage Publications.

Beattie, D.K. (2000) 'Creativity in art: the feasibility of assessing current conceptions in the school context', *Assessment in Education*, 7: 175–92.

Bunting, P. (2011), Realizing creative development, in N. Beach, J. Evans and G. Spruce (eds) *Making Music in the Primary School*, London: Routledge, pp. 107–15.

Burnard, P. (2009) 'Progression in musical composition', in H. Coll and A. Lamont (eds) *Sound Progress: Exploring musical development*, Derbyshire: National Association of Music Educators, pp. 73–8.

Burnard, P. and Younker, B.A. (2002), 'Mapping pathways: fostering creativity in composition, *Music Education Research*, 4(2): 245–61.

Campbell, P.S. (2000) 'What music really means to children', *Music Educators Journal*, 86(5): 32–6.

Casson, M. (2011) The creative process, in N. Beach, J. Evans and G. Spruce (eds) *Making Music in the Primary School*, London: Routledge, pp. 92–9.

Claxton, G. (2006) 'Thinking at the edge: soft creativity', *Cambridge Journal of Education*, 36(3): 351–62.

Claxton, G., Edwards, L. and Scale-Constantinou, V. (2006) 'Cultivating creative mentalities', *Thinking Skills and Creativity*, 1: 57–61.

Craft, A. (2000) *Creativity across the Primary Curriculum: framing and developing practice*, London: Routledge.

Craft, A. (2002) *Creativity and Early Years' Education: a life-wide foundation*, London: Continuum.

Cropley, A. (2001) *Creativity in Education and Learning: a guide for teachers and educators*, London: RoutledgeFalmer.

Crow, B. (2008) 'Changing conceptions of educational creativity: a study of student teachers' experience of musical creativity', *Music Education Research*, 10(3): 373–88.

Csikszentmihalyi, M. (1996) *Creativity: flow and the psychology of discovery and invention*, New York: HarperCollins.

Csikszentmihalyi, M. (1998) 'Creativity and genius: a systems perspective', in A. Steptoe (ed.) *Genius and Mind: studies of creativity and temperament*, New York: Oxford University Press, pp. 39–64.

Department for Children, Schools and Families (DCSF) (2003) *Excellence and Enjoyment: A strategy for primary schools*, London: DCSF.

Dineen, R. and Collins, E. (2005) 'Killing the goose: conflicts between pedagogy and politics in the delivery of a creative education', *Journal of Art and Design Education*, 24(1): 43–51.

Dunn, R.E. (1997). Creative thinking and music listening. *Research Studies in Music Education*, 8, 42–55.

Eisner, E.W. (1965) 'Children's creativity in art: a study of types', *American Educational Research Journal*, 2(3): 125–36.

Eisner, E.W. (1993) 'Forms of understanding and the future of educational research', *Educational Researcher*, 22(5): 5–11.

Eisner, E. (2002) *The Arts and the Creation of Mind*, New Haven: Yale University Press.

Ellison, J. and Creech, A. (2010) 'Music in the primary school', in S. Hallam and A. Creech (eds) *Music Education in the 21st Century in the United Kingdom: achievements, analysis and aspirations*, Institute of Education: University of London, pp. 211–27.

Fleming, M. (2010) *Arts in Education and Creativity: a literature review*, 2nd edn, London: Arts Council for England: Creativity, Culture and Education Series.

Gaut, B. and Livingston, P. (eds) (2003) *The Creation of Art*, Cambridge: Cambridge University Press.

Glück, J., Ernst, R. and Unger, F. (2002) 'How creatives define creativity: definitions reflect different types of creativity', *Creativity Research Journal*, 14(1), 55–67.

Hallam, S. (2006) *Music Psychology in Education*, Bedford Way Papers, London: Institute of Education, University of London.

Hallam, S. (2010) 'The power of music: its impact on the intellectual, personal and social development of children and young people', in S. Hallam and A. Creech (eds) *Music Education in the 21st Century in the United Kingdom: achievements, analysis and aspirations*, Institute of Education: University of London pp. 2–17.

Hallam, S., Burnard, P., Robertson, A., Saleh, C., Davies, V., Rogers, L. and Kokotsaki, D. (2009a) 'Trainee primary school teachers' perceptions of their effectiveness in teaching music', *Music Education Research*, 11(2): 221–40.

Hallam, S., Creech, A., Rinta, T. and Shave, K. (2009b) *EMI Music Sound Foundation: evaluation of the impact of additional training in the delivery of music at Key Stage 1: final report*, Institute of Education, University of London.

Hallam, S. and Rogers, L. (2010) 'Creativity', in S. Hallam and A. Creech (eds) *Music Education in the 21st Century in the United Kingdom: achievements, analysis and aspirations*, Institute of Education: University of London, pp. 105–22.

Hennessy, S. (2000) 'Overcoming the red-feeling: the development of confidence to teach music in primary school amongst student teachers', *British Journal of Music Education*, 17(2): 183–96.

Hennessy, S. (2006) 'Don't forget the teachers', *Times Educational Supplement, The Teacher*, March 24.

Hennessy, S. (2009) 'Creativity in the music curriculum', in A. Wilson (ed.) *Creativity in Primary Education*, Exeter: Learning Matters, pp. 134–47.

Hirsch, E.D. (1967) *Validity in Interpretation*, New Haven: Yale University.

Holden, H. and Button, S. (2006) 'The teaching of music in the primary school by the non-music specialist', *British Journal of Music Education*, 23(1): 23–38.

Jones, P. and Robson, C. (2008) *Teaching Music in Primary Schools*, Exeter: Learning Matters.

Jeffrey, B. and Woods, P. (2009) *Creative Learning in the Primary School*, London: Routledge.

Kokotsaki, D. (2011) 'Student teachers' conceptions of creativity in the secondary music classroom', *Thinking Skills and Creativity*, 6: 100–13.

Kokotsaki, D. (in press) 'Student-teachers' conceptions of creativity in the primary music classroom', *Research Studies in Music Education*.

Koutsoupidou, T. and Hargreaves, D.J. (2009) 'An experimental study of the effects of improvisation on the development of children's creative thinking in music', *Psychology of Music*, 37(3): 251–78.

Krathwohl, D.R. (2002) 'A revision of Bloom's taxonomy: an overview', *Theory into Practice*, 41(4): 212–65.

Kratus, J. (1990) 'Structuring the music curriculum for creative learning', *Music Educators Journal*, 76(9): 33–37.

Kyung, H.K. (2006) 'Can we trust creativity tests? A review of the Torrance Tests of Creative Thinking (TTCT)', *Creativity Research Journal*, 18(1): 3–14.

Lamont, A. (2001) *The Effects of Participating in Musical Activities*, Keele: Unit for the Study of Musical Skill and Development, Department of Psychology, Keele University. Online. Available at http://download-file.net/access.html (accessed 18 March 2011).

Lamont, A. (2008) 'Young children's musical worlds: musical engagement in 3.5-year-olds', *Journal of Early Childhood Research*, 6: 247–61.

Lanier, V. (1975) 'Objectives of art education', *Peabody Journal of Education*, 52: 180–6.

MacDonald, R., Byrne, C. and Carlton, L. (2006) 'Creativity and flow in musical composition: an empirical investigation', *Psychology of Music*, 34: 292–306.

Moore, J.L.S. (1990) 'Strategies for fostering creative thinking', *Music Education Journal*, 76(9): 38–42.

National Advisory Committee on Creative and Cultural Education Report (NACCCE) (1999) *All Our Futures: creativity, culture and education*, London: Department for Education and Employment.

Newton, D.P. and Donkin, H. (2011) 'Some notions of artistic creativity amongst history of art students acquired through incidental learning', *International Journal of Education through Art*, 7(3): 283–98.

Odena, O. (2001) 'Developing a framework for the study of teachers' views of creativity in music education', *Goldsmiths Journal of Education*, 4(1): 59–67.

Odena, O. and Welch, G. (2009) 'A generative model of teachers' thinking on musical creativity', *Psychology of Music*, 37(4): 416–42.

Office for Standards in Education (Ofsted) (2009) *Making More of Music: an evaluation of music in schools 2005–08* (No. 080235), London: Ofsted.

Osborne, T. (2003) '"Against creativity": a philistine rant', *Economy and Society*, 32(4): 507–25.

Prentice, R. (2000) 'Creativity: a reaffirmation of its place in early childhood education', *The Curriculum Journal*, 11: 145–58.

Qualifications and Curriculum Authority (QCA) (2005) *Music: 2004–05 Annual Report on Curriculum and Assessment*, London: QCA.

Qualifications and Curriculum Development Agency (QCDA) (2007) *Music at KS1 and KS2*, QCDA online. Available at: http://curriculum.qcda.gov.uk/key-stages-1-and-2/subjects/music/keystage1/index.aspx

Reimer, B. (1989) *A Philosophy of Music Education*, 2nd edn, Englewood Cliffs, NJ: Prentice-Hall.

Rose, J. (2009) *Independent Review of the Primary Curriculum* (No. 00499-2009DOM-EN), Nottingham: Department of Children, Schools and Families.

Ross, M. (1980) *The Arts and Personal Growth*, London: Pergamon Press.

Russell-Bowie, D. (1993) 'Where is music education in our primary schools? An examination of the current and practice of music education in NSW state primary schools', *Research Studies in Music Education*, 1: 52–8.

Russell-Bowie, D. (2009) 'What me? Teach music to my primary class? Challenges to teaching music in primary schools in five countries', *Music Education Research*, 11(1): 23–36.

Sawyer, R.K. (2006) 'Group creativity: musical performance and collaboration', *Psychology of Music*, 34(2): 148–65.

Seefeldt, C. (1995) 'Art – a serious work', *Young Children*, 50: 39–42.

Sharp, C. and Le Métais (2000), *The Arts, Creativity and Cultural Education: an international perspective*, London: Qualifications and Curriculum Authority.

Shillito, S., Beswick, K. and Baguley, M. (2008) 'The aims of art education', *Australian Online Journal of Arts Education*, 4(1): 1–16.

Siegemund, R. (1998) 'Why do we teach art today?' *Studies in Art Education*, 39(3): 197–214.

Sennett, R. (2008) *The Craftsman*, New Haven, CT: Yale University Press.

Sternberg, R.J. (2006) 'The nature of creativity', *Creativity Research Journal*, 18(1): 87–98.

Stricker, D.R. (2008) *Perceptions of Creativity in Art, Music and Technology Education*, Unpublished Ph.D. dissertation, Minnesota: University of Minnesota.

Swanger, D. (1990) 'Discipline-based art education', *Educational Theory*, 40(4): 437–42.

Swanwick, K. and Tillman, J. (1986) 'The sequence of musical development: a study of children's composition', *British Journal of Music Education*, 3(3): 305–39.

Thomas, T. (1991) 'Interart analogy: practice and theory in comparing the arts', *Journal of Aesthetic Education*, 25: 17–36.

United Nations Educational, Scientific and Cultural Organization (UNESCO) (2006) *Road Map for Arts in Education*. Lisbon: UNESCO.

Wallas, G. (1926) *The Art of Thought*, London: Watts.

Webster, P.R. (1990) 'Creativity as creative thinking', *Music Educators Journal*, 76(9): 22–8.

Webster, P. (2002) 'Creative thinking in music: advancing a model', in T. Sullivan and L. Willingham (eds) *Creativity and Music Education*. Toronto, Canada: Britannia Printers and Canadian Music Educators' Association, pp. 16–33.

Wilson, D. (2001) 'Guidelines for coaching student composers', *Music Educators Journal*, 88(1): 28–33.

Wolcott, A. (1996) 'Is what you see, what you get? A post-modern approach to understanding works of art', *Studies in Art Education*, 37: 69–79.

Wright, J. (1990) 'The artist, the art teacher, and misplaced faith: creativity and art education', *Art Education*, 43(6): 50–7.

Zbainos, D. and Anastasopoulou, A. (2008) 'The role of creative music activities in Greek compulsory education: An investigation of Greek music teachers' perceptions', Conference Proceedings of the 1st International Conference of the Institute for Excellence in Education: *Future Minds and Creativity*, Paris, 1–4 July.

Creativity in History and the Humanities

Anthony Blake and Gail Edwards

Introduction

Any discussion about creativity in history must begin with an understanding of history as a process and knowledge domain. Distinguishable from notions about the 'past', a conventional definition of the subject 'history' might be: knowledge about the past produced by historians based on the analysis of primary and secondary sources; it 'is about finding things out, and solving problems' and not 'about spinning narratives or telling stories' (Marwick 2001: 28–9). It would seem from this that there is not much room for creativity in history except perhaps in problem solving. Others, however, see history as more than this. For David Starkey (2005) history *is* the narrative construction of the past, 'a branch of storytelling'. For Hayden White history is 'story-shaped', where a particular 'emplotment' such as romance or tragedy is imposed on past events (Munslow 1997). Keith Hopkins (1999), writing about ancient Rome, argues that history is or should be a blend of empathetic imagination and critical analysis:

> We have to imagine what Romans … thought, felt, experienced, believed … So why then don't we incorporate this empathetic wonder, knowledge, pseudo-objective analysis, ignorance, competing assumptions and disagreements …?
>
> (Hopkins 1999: 2–3)

While history without such an evidence base may be unable to relay directly the emotions and lived experiences of people in the past, in the history classroom there is an opportunity for the imaginative act to fill in the gaps in the historical record to make events personally meaningful. This, of course, is the basis for historical representation in the Hollywood feature film which offers a plausible blend of historical evidence and imaginative invention to provide audiences with the means to re-experience the past and may, more critically, also offer an opportunity to 're-think' the past (Burgoyne 2008). History then in the primary classroom would seem to have the potential to be a creative process where children can use informed imagination to construct narratives and accounts of events and situations. Such an act is entirely in keeping with helping children recognize 'that the past is represented and interpreted in different ways, and to give reasons for this' [Department for Education and Employment (DfEE)/Qualifications and Curriculum Authority (QCA) 1999: 17].

The notion of creativity in history

Given that history is an interpretive, constructive discipline which draws upon imagination constrained by evidence about the past (Arnold 2000), it can be considered a creative activity. Creativity is at the heart of the historical endeavour and some argue persuasively that children should act as novice historians from the outset (Fines and Nichol 1997), although Mortimer (2008) would insist that children are best described as engaging in 'historical activity' rather than as 'historians'. Fines and Nichol compiled a sizeable evidence base attesting to the efficacy of initiating primary pupils into the process of 'doing history'. The emphasis here is on children engaging in authentic historical activity from which they construct their own 'histories' or stories of the past. This, they stress, is not to say that all stories are equally valid or that such stories constitute fiction; rather it is that young children's histories must be rooted in the historical record. This process requires children's imagination and creative thought, shaped by their lived experience.

Besides the construction of something 'new' or original, creativity also involves the creation of associative links, especially through inference. Here tentative explanations or understandings are constructed where the creative act: 'uncovers, selects, re-shuffles, combines and synthesizes already existing facts, ideas, faculties, skills' (Koestler in Turner-Bisset 2005: 14). Indeed, Cooper (1995) and Bage (2000) argue that most young children are capable of reconstructing the past from evidence, making unusual imaginative connections, tolerating ambiguity and engaging in 'possibility thinking'.

Sadly, a perception of elementary history teaching as transmitting uncontested truths – the outcomes of the disciplinary process – is still widespread (Turner-Bisset 2005). Many teachers may have had little exposure to the syntactic structures of history, the disciplinary process through which an explanation or narrative is constructed. This could shape their beliefs about history and how they teach it and so make teachers' conceptions of history and, in particular, school history in relation to their understandings about creativity important.

Trainee teachers' conceptions of creativity in history

Recent research carried out with 49 trainee teachers on a one-year Postgraduate Certificate of Education course leading to a qualification to teach 5–11-year-old children in England (Blake *et al.* 2011) explored their conceptions of creativity in history. Following the completion of a questionnaire, focus group interviews asked the pre-service teachers to:

- exemplify specific instances of history lessons observed or taught which they believed provided opportunities for children to be creative in history;

- clarify what children did which they considered was creative;

- identify what they considered to be worthy of high (and low) marks for creative behaviours in these lessons;

- explain the extent to which the taught component about enquiry in teaching history had influenced their views and practices regarding creativity in history; and

- discuss their views of obstacles to creative approaches to history in the primary school.

Adapting Marton's (1981) method of phenomographic analysis, responses were categorized with each group given a descriptive label, an account of its attributes and one or two examples to form a 'category of description'. Of course, the categories identified may not be all that exist: there could be more but, in practice, this is not an obstacle to learning something useful and informing discussion about these students' conceptions of historical creativity in the primary classroom.

Some background beliefs about creativity and history in the primary school curriculum

Although they recognized that history as a curriculum subject did involve creativity, other subjects such as English and Art were seen to offer more opportunities for creative thought on the part of the learners. Like history, these subjects were less rigidly structured with 'no right or wrong answers' and seen as offering more opportunity for individual thought, self-expression, interpretation, imagination and originality. Yet these other subjects were more open than history to a cross-curricular or a practical, 'hands-on' approach. In the primary school, opportunities for historical creativity could be recognized by the presence of drama/role play, creative writing, or 'hands-on' practical tasks involving problem-solving or making activities. Such history lessons were seen as a *vehicle* for creative writing or for enabling a cross-curricular approach to learning.

For others, the opportunity for imagination stemmed from historical reflection, interpretation, debate, imagining or employing independent thought and from empathy with those living in the past, or to make the past accessible or promote 'ownership' of it. For some, it was the opportunity these imaginative and practical elements gave children to interpret events in their own way ('putting their own slant on things'). Creativity was important because it motivated children and involved them directly and personally, it made them think, provided an opportunity for discussion which allowed children to come up with their own ideas, interpretation or to generate questions. For example, one student described her experience of using role play with children in the context of assessing insurance claims following the 1906 San Francisco earthquake. The task was to determine from photographic evidence the legitimacy of claims and to deliver the decision to the often traumatized survivors. The student felt that 'It was in their [the children's] hands, they picked the photos – child-led learning which is creative in its own way'. In another topic, a student recounted how, 'We took them on a journey as if they were going to the beach 50 years ago ... so we had a little Punch and Judy show set up and things they would have seen in those days and we got an old lady to come in dressed in clothes from those days and she talked to the children about what it was like when she was younger'. For these students, creative thought in history lessons was more than just learning about the past using documentary evidence, it was also about re-creating or re-experiencing the 'lived' past and, in effect, 'becoming' that historical person. For all the students, creative thinking in history meant more than just factual recall. While it could mean constructing explanations, it could also include motivation and feeling.

Categories of conceptions about creativity in the primary history classroom

It was evident that the students individually had varied understandings of creativity in history, and six categories of conception were identified. In the first, creativity was thought to be the means by which children can access the past in order to gain an empathetic understanding of how people lived and why they did the things they did; drama or role play allow us to experience what they experienced, in effect to 'become' them. Rather than as L.P. Hartley observed, the 'past is a foreign country' (quoted by Lowenthal 1985: xvi), here the past is knowable and recoverable, with people living in the past just like us.

The second category highlights the view that to imagine the past children must draw on the historical information and evidence made available to them by the teacher. In this sense their imagination in visioning the past or in constructing their own interpretation of it is constrained. The end-product must have plausibility, that is be consistent with the evidence and be justifiable within the limits and terms allowed by that evidence and information.

The third category shows an interest in pursuing facts, suggesting that to re-experience or interpret the past requires a necessary but relevant factual knowledge to draw upon. This is quite a different rationale to the non-creative approach to history with its exclusive focus on rote learning of factual content knowledge as the end-product rather than as the means to resolving 'historical questions'.

The fourth category sees creativity in the engineering of shared and positive feelings about the topic in history. This may conflate or confuse the creative act with its possible *effect* such as stimulating attention, generating interest and excitement, or in encouraging the children to want to find out or know more. Whilst enjoyment of a historical topic can act as an 'enquiring and critical force' according to Mortimer (2008: 457), a lesson which generates emotions is not necessarily one which stimulates creativity as Barrow and Woods (1975) observed some time ago in relation to science. It may also confuse a teacher's creativity with that of the children. Both of these would be misconceptions.

The fifth category proposes that for children to think creatively in history it is necessary for them to employ approaches and insights using a 'generic tool box' made up from, for example, drama, English, art and design and technology to solve problems. A cross-curricular approach was thus regarded as a mechanism which could 'reveal' the past to children and enable them to resolve problems in our understanding of the past as, for instance, in how Roman aqueducts 'worked' or how the Pyramids were constructed.

In the sixth category, creativity permits children to make sense of, and explain the past. Here the pre-service teachers came closest to the notion that history is a discipline which allows for the different explanations and interpretations. The children's own interpretations may not provide original historical accounts or be acceptable to the community of historians, but the child's interpretation provides an explanation which may be *new to them*. In both these categories, the use of imagination to construct a mental image to experience or interrogate the past is central to creative thought in the history classroom.

Creativity and history: three different perspectives

Taken together, these beliefs suggest three different perspectives or orientations concerning how the relationship between creativity and history is conceptualized. Each perspective reflects particular notions about desired outcomes and the history curriculum, and about how the relationship between the past and history is understood. While new teachers' notions are consistent with general and more specific views about creativity in the history classroom, most conceptions were found to equate more with creativity *in* history or approaches *to* history, than creative thinking *about* history. We would argue that these perspectives are relevant to any primary teacher who aims to encourage creative thought through his or her teaching of history.

The first perspective might be described as *creativity in history*. Here, history is seen as a curriculum subject much like any other, to be judged on the basis of its potential as a *vehicle* to promote creativity as an end in itself. Outcomes in this perspective are concerned with the creative product or act rather than with an understanding of the past. For example, with older primary children a teacher might ask the class to design a mechanism to lift tubs of coal from underground up to the surface of a Victorian coalmine.

The second perspective might be described as *creative approaches to history*. Here, generic creative approaches from English, drama, art, and design and technology are used to *deliver* the history curriculum. It views the past and history as essentially the same. Outcomes show concern for the transmission of a relatively known and agreed past consistent with the goals of the National Curriculum: chronological understanding, knowledge and understanding of events, people and change; historical interpretation and the skills of enquiry (DfEE/QCA 1999). Enquiry is seen *ultimately* as a means of generating explanations largely in line with reaching a pre-defined, shared or agreed understanding of events and people. For example, a teacher might ask the children to contrast the lives of rich and poor in the Victorian era using paintings and photographs with a view to them reaching an understanding of the contrasting experiences of these groups.

The third perspective might be called *creative thinking about history*. Here, the past and history are different; history is a construction of an essentially unknowable or contested truth about events and personalities in the past, so no single account constructed by historians can ever be final. That different interpretations are possible, so long as they are plausible and accord with the available evidence, provides the conceptual basis for exploring the past. Outcomes focus on the children constructing a credible account, original to themselves, which they are then able to justify. Enquiry is seen as important and more as a *process* than as a means to reaching a pre-defined, shared or agreed understanding of events and people. In this case, Key Stage 2 children might enact a courtroom scene which presents evidence for alternative and conflicting judgements with regard to historical events and personalities. They might, for example, undertake a 'mock' trial with judge and jury to decide if Lee Harvey Oswald assassinated President Kennedy, or whether Henry VIII was a 'bloodthirsty tyrant'.

These perspectives are not mutually exclusive and many teachers, like the student teachers here, are likely to hold multiple perspectives, although one could be dominant. A number of the students appeared to prioritize history as a *vehicle* for creativity. Perhaps this may reflect a particular interpretation of initiatives which promote creativity through a cross-curricular approach to the primary curriculum [DfEE/QCA 1999; Craft 2002; Department for Education and Skills (DfES) 2003]. But most students saw history lessons as more than this, providing opportunities for children to gain a better understanding of the past by acting as 'novice historians' (Fines and Nichol 1997) through enquiry or problem-solving approaches. Few students, however, appeared to conceptualize the link between creativity and history as being creative thinking *about* history. It is tempting to think that this is what the some students meant when they claimed that creativity involved the opportunity for children to give their own 'slant' or interpretation, or when one student observed that creativity involved, 'The ability to represent "Ancient" Rome in the eyes of a modern person without losing sight of its "Ancient" nature'. However, none of the students interviewed made reference to history itself as a *construction* offering the possibility of different interpretations, but only to the possibility for children to give a *personal* view. Rather, interviews confirmed the view that the dominant perspective held by most students related to creative approaches *to* history. These students wanted the children to develop a meaningful understanding of the past, to identify personally with people in the past and understand why they lived or behaved the way they did. Collectively, the students saw creativity almost exclusively in relation to teaching and learning about a 'fixed' or 'closed', relatively unproblematic, past that is both known and knowable. Based, in the main, on such a perspective, teaching history then becomes the process of delivering uncontested truths about the past revealed by historians. According to Turner-Bisset (2005), creative approaches have tended to foster such a view in primary schools.

Fostering creative thinking in history

The research discussed above suggests that, as well as appreciating creativity *in* and *to* history, a richer understanding of the creative potential of history by teachers and pupils also requires their appreciation of the constructed and contestable nature of historical knowledge (i.e. creative thinking *about* history). Essentially this means that children should be initiated into the critical and imaginative thinking of the historical community and this in turn demands that their teachers are competent historical enquirers, able to model and scaffold this process of construction and contestation. And of course, in teachers and pupils, this ability to investigate the past, search for clues, draw conclusions and imaginatively bring the past to life, in turn comes from working with experts, such as history teacher educators, academics or professional historians.

So what does this look like in practice? Essentially, the principles of historical enquiry include consideration of protocols, curiosity and challenge, and the key concepts of evidence and interpretation. These are now considered in turn.

Protocols

If we take the view that the role of a historian involves a form of storytelling (i.e. producing accounts of the past based on imagination and evidence), then a 'protocol' is essential (Nichol and Dean 1997). A protocol acts as an analytic frame for the experience to follow and takes the form of a role to which the children are assigned. There are many roles children may play – archaeologist, archivist, museum curator or film-maker are just a few possibilities – and the type of protocol will influence both the audience and the form the historical account subsequently takes.

For example, during the history component of a postgraduate initial teacher training course, the students undertook an enquiry which might easily be undertaken by schoolchildren and which involves a protocol. The enquiry began with the telling of a story about a local girl. The tale was the tutor's own creation, put together using evidence drawn from a range of archival sources. It was an emotive story which recounted the events leading up to the death of the young girl, Lizzie Dowson, who died from ingesting lead when working in a Victorian leadworks. What remains of the leadworks and Lizzie's home are situated locally, within walking distance of the university and the enquiry included a visit there to identify the primary sources relating to Lizzie's life. At the outset, the students were not told how or why Lizzie died but invariably the story provoked consternation and ultimately led to the question around which the subsequent enquiry was structured: *Who or what was to blame for the death of Lizzie Dowson?* At this point, the students were assigned the role of historians making up committees of inquiry charged with the responsibility of investigating the cause(s) of Lizzie's death. The protocol here brings in purpose and audience; each committee group knew that they had to produce a credible report for their peers – an historical narrative which outlined their conclusions based upon evidence, reason, empathy and imagination. The intention here was to help the students understand how protocols act as framing devices, introducing ambiguity, imagination and open-endedness into learning yet within a purposive structure. These are key features of situations demanding creativity in the sense we define it here; the contested nature of historical knowledge is made clear since the transmission of (final) unequivocal knowledge about the past is discouraged.

Challenge

Initiating or inducting children into quality historical thinking involves supporting their construction of the past through investigation. This poses a considerable challenge for both teacher and children. The protocol discussed above helps, since it acts as a frame – and a scaffold – for the asking of historical questions. In the Lizzie Dowson enquiry, the student teachers acted as historians in asking questions related to key historical concepts such as chronology (*When did Lizzie die?*), change (*What was changing then and how?*), causation (*Why did Lizzie die?*) and significance (*Why was this event important?*), but the answers to these questions are of course never final. This constructivist pedagogy is not innocent for it carries its own message. Not only do the students learn something here about historical learning but they also learned an epistemological lesson. Since the answers to their questions had to be rooted in the historical record, supplemented with imagination and empathy, they learned something about the social construction of knowledge.

Just as children might also do if given a similar task, they learned that history is the production of contested narrative. The enquiry-based approach thus puts into action Bruner's (1960) spiral curriculum and Dewey's (1997) exhortation to treat 'end points' as provisional new beginnings.

Key concepts of evidence and interpretation

Evidence and interpretation are key ingredients in creating accounts of the past. At the outset of their enquiry, it was evident that the student teachers were more comfortable with using history textbooks than with the use of authentic historical sources. Textbooks of course can give the illusion of presenting an unproblematic historical record and may be believed to be 'safe' by student teachers who understand the history curriculum as uncontested content to be delivered. In the Lizzie Dowson enquiry, however, the student teachers are required to interrogate a range of sources. Such interrogation of primary and secondary sources leads them to experience uncertainty, ambiguity and contestation. Whilst this may at times be uncomfortable, these are all intellectual virtues associated with creativity. Of course, textbooks too, along with film and television drama, artworks and historical fiction are also useful sources of evidence. Gradually the student teachers recognize that children can, given sufficient support, engage critically with such sources. Some further ideas for encouraging creative thinking in history are provided in Table 6.1.

Some student teachers found the demands placed upon their interpretive, critical and imaginative faculties disconcerting. This occasionally leads to scepticism regarding the capabilities of young children to engage with sources in this way. However, this view soon diminishes as they continue on their journey, experiencing at first hand the historical process. The exhilaration and sense of creative accomplishment that comes with constructing and defending interpretations of the past within a community of historians, is enough to make the challenge worthwhile.

Fostering creative thinking in geography

The key principles of *protocol*, *curiosity* and *challenge* can also be helpful in framing our thinking about creativity in geography. Geography, like history, is concerned with constructing understanding. Geographers seek to understand the interaction of people and their environment (Smeaton 1998). Understanding a locality – particularly if it is a distant place and has not been visited first hand – relies upon children's ability to extrapolate from sources as well as the application of imagination and vicarious thinking. Moreover, controversial issues in geography, such as conflicts over land-use, for example, demand an ability to appraise and empathize with competing perspectives and motives (Hicks 1998).

The protocol or analytic frame in a geographical enquiry is important. Children could be assigned the role of environmentalist, town planner, travel book writer, or explorer. The possibilities are almost limitless and an enquiry may even incorporate a combination of roles. Just as with history, it is important that children have an audience and goal to

TABLE 6.1 Some ideas to promote creativity in history through enquiry

YEAR	ENGAGING CURIOSITY	PROTOCOL	ACTIVITIES	AUDIENCE OR GOAL
Nursery/reception	Find an old box full of toys – who did it belong to? As a class, unwrap one toy at a time and speculate!	Be museum curators responsible for creating a new Toy Museum in school which shows how toys have changed over the years.	Visit a real museum; explore information texts, photographs, and old and new toys. Listen to an oral account of an older person as they explain how they played when they were children.	Toy Museum display with labels, artefacts and a museum guidebook, prepared for other children in school to visit.
Year 1	Tell part of the story of Florence Nightingale. Who was she? What happened to her?	Act as history detectives to find out why she is remembered.	Listen to stories, watch recreations of her life, visit a museum and explore artefacts from the period.	Produce a class book of her story.
Year 2	Story told from the point of view of a child evacuee.	Act as history film-makers charged with the responsibility of making a short film about the evacuees of WW2.	Research using secondary sources and oral history. Role play, filming, editing and producing the film.	A documentary film for other children in school, which could be shared during assembly.
Year 3	Listen to a story about the Viking raids. Were the Vikings really vicious?	Form a committee of enquiry with responsibility for answering the key question.	Interrogating a range of secondary sources – visual and textual. Examine replica artefacts from the past for clues as to the Viking raids.	Presentation to the class with the aim of providing the most convincing and well-supported answer to the question.

Year 4	Find an old suitcase in school or in somebody's loft. Who did it belong to?	Act as local historians to find out about this person who lived in our locality in the past.	Local history study based around the story of the suitcase owner.	Create a book for the local library or history study centre.
Year 5	Begin with the story of the beheading of Anne Boleyn. What led to this dramatic event? Was it right to behead this woman?	Act as historians to investigate the Tudor period to uncover the reasons behind Henry VIII's actions.	Research using a range of secondary sources, including written accounts, visual accounts and replica artefacts. Role play key scenes.	Enact these dramatic events in assembly in a performance created for other children in school.
Year 6	Tell the story of the curse of Tutankhamen. Could it be true?	Act as journalists charged with the responsibility of writing an history article for the local newspaper.	Interrogate the evidence for and against the truth of the story.	Create a newspaper report which can be included in a local newspaper or magazine.

TABLE 6.2 Some ideas to promote creativity in geography through enquiry

YEAR	ENGAGING CURIOSITY	PROTOCOL	ACTIVITIES	AUDIENCE OR GOAL
Nursery/reception	Barnaby has sent a letter to the class, asking them if their area is a nice place to visit for his holidays. Can they help Barnaby?	Act as Barnaby's helpers by telling him what our local area is like.	Go on a walk around the school. Look for things in the environment we like and things we don't.	Write a letter or make a video to show Barnaby the things we like about our local area.
Year 1	Listen to the story *Katie Morag and the two grandmothers* by Mairi Hedderwick (Bodley Head, hardback, Red Fox, paperback and big book). What is it like to live on an island?	Act as film-makers to make a video of life in our own locality and how it is different to Katie's life.	Listen to stories, watch video of island life, make collage maps and pictures of Struay. Examine photographs of the Isle of Coll in the Inner Hebrides.	Produce a film of life in our locality to show the audience what makes our locality distinctive.
Year 2	Read a letter to the class from the local planner at the council. There may be a new road built through the village. What do the children think about this?	Act as town planners to decide whether the new road should go ahead.	Investigate the local area to see what the new road would affect. Who would benefit? What do local people think?	Produce a display in school to show what would be lost and what would be gained by the building of a new road.
Year 3	Show a newspaper report of an incidence of pollution (could be real or imaginary and concerned with water, air or land pollution). Why is this happening here?	Form a committee of enquiry with the responsibility of answering the key question.	Interrogating a range of secondary sources – maps, witness accounts, reports and other evidence.	Presentation to the class with the aim of providing the most convincing and well-supported answer to the question.

Year 4	Read a story which recounts the difficulties of the Adivasi people in Chembakolli Why is their way of life threatened?	Act as journalists charged with the responsibility for writing a report on the Adivasi people for the school or local magazine, to raise awareness.	Locality study based on Chembakolli in the Nilgiri Hills area of India. (Photopacks and artefacts are available for this locality study.)	Write a class report which explains the point of view of the Adivasi people.
Year 5	Tell the story of the death of Iqbal, a slave who worked in a carpet factory in Pakistan, who campaigned for civil rights and then was murdered (available from the Internet).	Act as detectives to discover why Iqbal was killed and why some children work in factories in India.	Research using a range of secondary sources, including written accounts, visual accounts and Internet sources.	Produce an assembly which raises awareness of child labour in other parts of the world.
Year 6	Show children a video or news report about a current or recent event – such as a volcanic eruption, earthquake flooding, desertification, etc.	Children act as geographers to find out the causes and details behind the event.	Research using a range of resources – maps, photographs, reports, etc.	Create their own video to show to other children which explains the causes and details of the event.

give shape and purpose to their investigation. One example, explored by postgraduate students of an initial teacher training course, involved Key Stage 1 children in evaluating a local coastal area for its suitability as a retirement location for an ageing Barnaby Bear. The enquiry involved fieldwork in the locality as well as the critical examination of various secondary sources of information in the classroom. The enquiry concluded with a letter to Barnaby outlining the advantages and disadvantages of the area as a retirement location.

Over the primary phase, such enquiries could be designed to complement the three interrelated aspects of study which constitute geography in the National Curriculum: place, skills and themes. Curiosity, of course, must drive these geographical enquiries and some examples of strategies to stimulate children's desire to know are given in Table 6.2. These act as a scaffold to assist children in the asking of geographical questions. These questions lead to the development of key geographical concepts such as location (*Where is this place/issue?*), interconnectedness (*How is this place connected to other places?*), sense of place (*What is it like?*), human and physical processes (*How did it come to be like this?*) and values (*What do I think about it?*). Since the answers to these questions must be rooted in the evidence available, supplemented with imagination and empathy, children learn important epistemological lessons about the construction of geographical knowledge and the study of geography itself.

In conclusion

To encourage creative thinking in the humanities, teachers need to avoid seeing creativity as only a descriptive or fact-finding, technological problem-solving, emotion-enhancing event, an opportunity for creativity *per se*. It is important that they recognize that creativity in history is multidimensional encompassing creative thinking *about* history as well as creative approaches *to* history. These principles also apply to the study of geography. As we have argued above, to support children's understanding about history and geography, teachers must themselves be committed historical and geographical enquirers who are able to model and scaffold this process of construction and contestation.

References

Arnold, J.H. (2000) *History*, Oxford: Oxford University Press.
Bage, G. (2000) *Thinking History 4–14*, London, RoutledgeFalmer.
Barrow, R. and Woods, R. (1975) *An Introduction to Philosophy of Science*, 2nd edn, London: Methuen.
Blake, A., Edwards, G., Newton, D.P. and Newton, L.D. (2011) 'Some students conceptions of creativity in primary school history', *International Journal of Historical Learning Teaching and Research*, 9(2): 15–24.
Bruner, J. (1960) *The Process of Education*, London: Harvard University Press.
Burgoyne, R. (2008) *The Hollywood Historical Film*, Oxford: Blackwell Publishing.
Cooper, H. (1995) *The Teaching of History in Primary Schools*, 2nd edn, London: David Fulton.
Craft, A. (2002) *Creativity and Early Years Education*, London: Continuum.
Department for Education and Employment (DfEE)/Qualifications and Curriculum Authority (QCA) (1999) *National Curriculum for England: History*, London: DfEE/QCA.

Department for Education and Skills (DfES) (2003) *Excellence and Enjoyment: learning and teaching in the primary years*, London: DfES.

Dewey, J. (1997) *How We Think*, New York: Dover Publications.

Fines, J. and Nichol, J. (1997) *Teaching Primary History*, Oxford: Heinemann.

Hicks, D. (1998) Exploring futures, in Carter, R. (ed.) *Handbook of Primary Geography*, Sheffield: The Geographical Association.

Hopkins, K. (1999) *A World Full of Gods*, London: The Free Press.

Lowenthal, D. (1985) *The Past is a Foreign Country*, Cambridge: Cambridge University Press.

Marton, F. (1981) 'Phenomenography – describing conceptions of the world around us', *Instructional Science*, 10: 177–200.

Marwick, A. (2001) *The New Nature of History: knowledge, evidence, language*, London: Palgrave.

Mortimer, I. (2008) 'What isn't history? The nature and enjoyment of history in the twenty-first century', *History*, 93: 454–74.

Munslow, A. (1997) *Deconstructing History*, London: Routledge.

Nichol, J. and Dean, J. (1997) *History 7–11 Developing primary teaching skills*, London: Routledge.

Smeaton, M. (1998) 'Questioning geography', in Carter, R. (ed.) *Handbook of Primary Geography*, Sheffield: The Geographical Association.

Starkey, D. (2005) 'History in British Education. What history should we be teaching in Britain in the 21st century?' *Institute of Historical Research Conference, University of London, 14–15 February*. Online. Available at: http://www.history.ac.uk/resources/history-in-british-education/first-conference (accessed 6 October 2009).

Turner-Bisset, R. (2005) *Creative Teaching: History in the primary classroom*, London: David Fulton.

7

Exploring Creativity within ICT: Concepts, Themes and Practices

Caroline Walker and Alan Gleaves

Introduction

In the twenty-first century, the fostering of creativity is considered essential in most school curricula. In an era seemingly dominated by curriculum models centred upon their contribution to 'the knowledge society', creativity has grown to have such importance that it is now considered critical for personal relationships, professional development, employment enhancement and economic prosperity (Banaji and Burn 2007). The importance of fostering children's creativity is well established (Fasko 2001; Odena and Welch 2009; Van Damme 2009) and research demonstrates that across all education sectors, from the very early years (Simge 2010) to primary education (Kampylis, Berki and Saariluoma 2009) through compulsory schooling (Jimoyiannis and Komis 2007) to post compulsory (Gomoluch and Whittaker 2007) and higher education (Walker and Gleaves 2008), there is an increasing concern with pedagogic practices that help develop learners' creativity. Much research suggests that teachers' practices make a critical contribution to the development of children's creativity, Kampylis, Berki and Saariluoma (2009) arguing that teachers are expected both to model creative pedagogies and grow creativity in pupils' and students' minds from their earliest possible classroom encounters.

Information and communications technology (ICT) is in an almost unique position with regard to the development of creativity: it is seen by educationalists as both a means and a process to innovate within education at large (Banaji and Burn 2007) as well as being a precursor to pupils' longer term development of metacognitive skills such as analysis, evaluation, reflection and reflexivity (Wheeler *et al.* 2002). Owing to the almost unique construction of what is regarded as 'disciplinary' ICT, from music composition, to film production, from programming applications to constructing critiques on social networks, ICT affords opportunities to 'create' according to almost every definition of creativity. As such, ICT is believed by many teachers and learners alike to be the critical element of any curriculum that will confer an innovative mind set that is 'attuned to the needs of the knowledge society' (Devolder *et al.* 2010: 1651).

However, there are several aspects of the relationship between ICT and creativity that are problematic, and it is these that will be discussed within this chapter. The first concerns the common conflation of, and confusion between, ICT-related creativity and digital creativity within education and schools generally (Fasko 2001; Sang *et al.* 2010) and the trajectory of their respective developments. Second, as Hermans *et al.* (2008) point out, despite the omnipresence of relatively cheap technology, there is a tangible gap between innovatory vision and actual practice in many educational settings because of the conceptual and structural impediments to understanding and incorporating ICT and digital media that will facilitate and develop creativity. Third, as a result of this technological and curricula confusion, questions of how teachers may harness the potential of ICT and digital media for developing creative skills transferable to real-life situations persist in almost all sectors of schooling and education. Much of this confusion rests on both teachers' and pupils' experiences with technology in both formal and informal settings. The aim of this chapter is to examine these issues in depth, particularly comparing the beliefs of teachers and how these relate to their practices of developing pupils' creativity within the ICT classroom. As such, it has the potential to provide information regarding teacher initial and professional development in ICT as well as contributing to the literature on creativity within the context of ICT classrooms.

Understanding the trajectory of innovation and creativity within ICT

According to the United Nations Educational, Scientific and Cultural Organization (UNESCO) handbook on *ICT in Schools* (2005: 15):

> The world's most serious problems – the growing demand for food, shelter, health, employment, and quality of life – cannot be solved without highly efficient new technologies. With the advantages of being nature-protecting, non-polluting, less energy consuming, and more human-friendly, ICT applications are becoming indispensable parts of contemporary culture, spreading across the globe through general and vocational education.

Aside from these global aspirations, the educational potential of ICT is equally stressed at individual pupil and classroom level (Becker 2000; Cooper and Brna 2002). For instance, Hosgorur and Bilasa (2009) stress the potential of ICT to:

- present rich learning environments, allowing learners to adopt multiple perspectives on complex phenomena;
- foster flexible knowledge construction in complex learning domains; and
- facilitate inclusion through the personalization of subject material.

Yet despite the clear and unequivocal importance attached to ICT within diverse research contexts, economists and educationalists alike assert that the use and application of ICT is a double-edged sword that may ultimately impede human development because of unequal distribution of particular ICT-related skills. According to UNESCO, what will ultimately prevent this happening is the preparation of a whole generation of teachers who can ensure that, 'ICTs are in the possession of people who use them creatively and for the common good' (UNESCO 2005: 14). However, the trajectory of ICT and its relationship with creativity demonstrate that progress toward this aim has frequently been slow and incoherent and with many impediments to its full realization remain.

ICT was introduced as an English National Curriculum (NC) subject at secondary level 15 years ago, following the 1995 revision of the NC. As a result, the training of specialist information technology (IT) teachers began in 1997. Prior to this, IT had appeared in the NC as 'IT capability', a strand of the Technology curriculum and computers were only used by a limited number of teachers (Plomp and Pelgrum 1991) and the integration of computers in the majority of school subjects was extremely limited. Much of the published research into the use of ICT and Learning Technology in Education at the time was focused either on the adoption and incorporation of what was then termed simply 'Information Technology' into schools at a broad institutional level or conversely on the efficacy of particular software for very specific individual disciplinary uses (Drent and Meelissen 2008).

Both of these mechanisms offer important perspectives from which to view the development of innovation and creativity within ICT. With the adoption and incorporation of IT into schools, a great deal of innovation was carried out, but in two seemingly polarized ways: from the outside in, as in the case of Local Authority Advisory Teachers; or, contrastingly, from a frequently idiosyncratic perspective of inside out, as in the case of science teachers turned programmers, or frequently, commerce teachers turned IT trainers. As Plomp and Pelgrum (1991) asserted, although the numbers of schools equipped with computers and the number of computers available in schools had increased dramatically over the decade 1980–1990, such gains had simply not been transferred to pupils in any coherent curriculum or pedagogic sense. Most innovation and creativity at classroom level rested on the enthusiasm and skill of a few individual teachers who were effectively 'technology entrepreneurs', fostering creativity amongst pupils through a mixture of modelling and iterative 'enrichment' using the children's own informally gained expertise (see e.g. the work of Wheeler *et al.* 2002; Pearson and Naylor 2006). The consequent development of creative pedagogies or activities within ICT became (and arguably still is) a function of culture and social discourse to a much greater degree than in other disciplines.

This scenario is illustrated well within the primary sector, where the introduction and implementation of ICT within the NC has been closely associated with 'change agents', individuals who create and creatively adapt resources and learning contexts, utilizing the most recent technologies (Devolder *et al.* 2010). Owing to the continual technological innovation and improvement within schools (e.g. the local authority Grids for Learning) and the more recent growth in use of *virtual learning environments* (VLEs), schools have grown to rely on such change agents, people who can guide and support the school during the process of implementing ICT into education. Within primary schools, this role has been usually assigned to an ICT coordinator, also known as the technology or computer coordinator (Lai *et al.* 2002). The ICT coordinator plays an important role in the integration and management of ICT in primary schools, and according to Devolder *et al.* (2010), the majority of teachers cannot facilitate learning and teaching without the support of such a person.

What is significant in these two contrasting educational contexts is the importance of a single individual in understanding innovation and creativity within ICT, a situation that largely remains in current teachers' practices within schools. This is illustrated well in terms of the trajectory of teacher preparation in ICT. Writing in 1993, Oliver asserted that beginning teachers who received formal training in the use of ICT did not differ in their future use of computers for teaching from those not receiving such training. Furthermore, individual creativity and innovation in the classroom appeared to be a function of both individual inclination and expertise, almost invariably gained in informal contexts. Almost two decades later, Haydn and Barton (2007) and Hammond *et al.* (2009) conducted studies that had very similar findings. In short, the propensity to be creative and innovate in ICT classrooms very much exists on an individual basis and is frequently a function of previous experience, ongoing professional opportunities for individual innovation and interpretation of emerging curricula. Indeed, Drent and Meelissen (2008) emphasize the significance of so-called 'pedagogic entrepreneurs' in integrating ICT into the curriculum, even suggesting that school level factors are of limited importance in enhancing teachers' own long-term creativity and innovation in ICT. This concept of 'personal entrepreneurship' is perhaps most evident in the domain of 'digital creativity'.

Introducing the concept of digital creativity

In December 2006 the European Parliament and the Council released the 'Recommendation on Key Competences for Lifelong Learning', where a new frame-work for key competences was outlined, encompassing ethical, cognitive and techno-logical dimensions that could be integrated to produce the complex concept of 'digital competence' (Calvani *et al.* 2008). The emerging idea was clear: traditional educational frameworks centred on the minimum goals of competent literacy and numeracy achieve-ments within schools must reform, to prepare citizens amongst other things, to be 'future-proof'. Perhaps the most significant element of such futuristic education would be particular abilities and skills developed under the umbrella of 'digital competence'. One such ability would be 'digital creativity', a twenty-first century imperative that many would argue has replaced manufacturing and industry as both the raw material and means of production of economic growth, and personal empowerment.

The meaning and significance of digital creativity within the centralized NC in the UK is both complex and contested, and is according to Banaji, Burn and Buckingham (2010), a matter of balancing diverse rhetorics. One such rhetoric is the economic one, which suggests that digital creativity has a clear productive purpose. For example, Scholtz and Livingstone (2005) suggest an unproblematic link between technology, creativity and learning, asserting that creativity resides 'naturally' within most digital technology use, implicitly invoking Constructivist pedagogy. Another rhetoric concerns self-realization: for example, in 2009, the Organization for Economic Cooperation and Development

(OECD) emphasized the relationship between pupils' learning about and through digital technology and later skills-based flexibility, personal empowerment and employability (see Taddei 2009). Finally, there is a 'social rhetoric' for digital creativity, in which educationalists seek to capitalize on the socially experienced and situated nature of digital creativity. This rhetoric is predicated on the fact that within the twenty-first century lives of most children in the UK, experience and situatedness manifests itself as extensive familiarity both with the moving image (film, television and video), and with digital means of producing and manipulating digital media (mobile devices, phones, cameras). However, Selwyn and Bullon (2000) assert that, since this capability with digital media is increasingly an important source of social capital and a prerequisite for participation in both society and the workplace, there are necessities within ICT curricula to ensure not just equitable access to the means of being digitally creative, but also to those that foster the higher level abilities to use cognition and interaction to be a digital creator. It is important to point out that many of these pedagogical arguments are made on the basis of the virtue of there being 'digital natives', a new generation of youth supposedly in possession of fluency with the mechanics and grammar of digital media and associated technologies. For example, the UK Government's Department for Business Innovation and Skills (BIS) report, *Digital Britain: Final Report* (BIS 2009: 1) states:

> Digital creativity comprises the skills and knowledge to utilize new digital technologies in the creative process. Creativity defines our future world and is a distinguisher in wealth creation and sustainability. The challenge for policymakers is to harness this new power in a positive way. It's time for Britons to get digital.

However, viewing the notion of naturally sophisticated 'digital creatives' through a critical lens, such rhetoric appears less convincing. Indeed, according to Buckingham (2007) and Carr (2008), there is a tendency amongst some teachers to assume that moving-image media devalue and detract from 'real' education because such media use, although superficially creative, is informal, recreational and low level. Arguably, such a state of affairs is reinforced by the continual exhortations of teachers and educators to police young people in formal networked environments so comprehensively that they limit any possibility of deeper engagement with diverse forms of what Stern (2008) has termed 'digital behaviour'. In actual fact, as Buckingham (2007) and Hosgurur and Bilasa (2009) point out, young people's informal digital media use may not only be extremely technically complex, but also quite simply incomparable with that in a formal curriculum. Studies also demonstrate that many teachers have contrary views about the creativity of digital media use, suggesting that, although somewhat technically difficult, skill is more easily developed because creative activities carried out in those contexts, such as film-making using YouTube, or music-producing using Garage Band, are innately pleasurable. Research in the field of gaming (see e.g. Arnone *et al.* 2009), where complex problem solving is frequently associated with high levels of creativity, suggests otherwise, however: young people testify to the frustration, pain and endless repetition and practice needed to become experts in particular gaming contexts.

The research suggests therefore that the reality of digital creativity is somewhat messy. While appearing to have highly technical competence and superficially creative dispositions in digital media production and use, Li and Ranieri (2010) suggest that many young people are unable to 'read' such media at a deeper level and, rather than being able to create and critique digital texts, can only re-produce and consume them, suggesting that 'digital nativity' and 'digital creativity' may well be mutually exclusive. On the other hand, being a member of a digital community where the level of analysis and technical ability required is directly related to social capital acquired as a result of belonging, demonstrates a strategic creativity that has personal empowerment and particular ability dimensions (Sefton Green and Sinker 2000).

Consequently, in any discussion of ICT and digital creativity, it is important to distinguish between ICT as a curriculum subject, ICT as a cross-curricular learning tool, ICT as an educational strategy, ICT as a teaching enhancement activity, ICT as a proxy for informal learning, and digital technology as a discipline or a means of production. Here, the concern is with teaching that might foster children's own creativity in the most broadly defined way, in other words, the central issue concerns the determination of what counts as ICT creativity in actual classrooms.

So what counts as creativity and creative practice within ICT?

Creativity has its definitional complexities, scholars in the field having theorized two major types. The first broadly defined in terms of individual attributes and contributions (Sak 2004), its measure of expression being the contribution to society. The second type is conceptualized as an innate human quality (Ward *et al.* 1999), being expressed through opportunities to experiment, collaborate, and ultimately express the nature of what it is to be human. Maslow (1962) distinguished 'special talents' and 'self actualization', Nicholls (1972) described a continuum of creativity from 'eminent' to 'everyday', Gardner (1993) advocated the significance of 'big C' and 'little c' creativity, whilst Davies (2006) has debated the pedagogic implications of 'elite' and 'democratic' interpretations.

ICT occupies a puzzling place in such discussions of creativity. Wheeler *et al.* (2002) have suggested that the diverse concepts that constitute ICT require a unique model of creativity predicated upon three discrete but related modes of activity: problem solving, creative cognition, and social interaction. However, as Buckingham (2007) points out, a cursory glance at the ICT and digital technology-based creative industries suggests that most employees utilize 'small c' creativity, carrying out mundane tasks with limited autonomy. It is the nature of human expression and 'self actualization' that intersect clearly in the realm of digital creativity, where particular technologies assist individuals in the deconstruction of assumptions made about them and others, through information, through communication, and through access. Rather than facilitating ever more unquestioning knowledge acquisition, as Carr (2008) suggests, Sanz and Romero (2007) assert that creativity in ICT use is concerned with the critique of information and digital media, in order that children can better understand the versions and subversions of the complex culture surrounding them. In agreement, Banaji, Burn and Buckingham (2010) suggest that digital creativity is the process of externalizing human identity through the visibility and multiple modes of representation afforded by media texts.

In other words, the creativity necessitated within the vocational application of ICT and digital technology is quite different to that used within informal learning contexts, but both are important given the centrality of ICT and digital technology in the twenty-first century. Despite these conceptual contrasts, however, the literature demonstrates that across all ages of education, in differing cultural contexts, there appears to be a disjunction between how these ideas are represented in ICT curricula and what teachers ultimately decide to do that can be described as 'creative ICT' in practice, whether through teaching or enhancement of the learning environment.

Within the early years and primary education curriculum, the greatest emphasis on creativity in and with ICT lies in the realms of play, socialization, understanding children's worlds and story-telling, as exemplified by Turvey's (2006) case study of participatory learning through shared online communities, Graham's (2009) work on digital representations of autobiography as themes in children's authored literature, and Loveless' (2003) inquiry into the possibilities of using digital media creatively across the humanities curriculum. Since a persistent justification for the ubiquity of digital creativity within the primary curriculum in particular concerns children's literacy and cognitive development, it is perhaps unsurprising that so much of ICT's creative potential is centred upon communication and the exploration of narratives – whether personal, historical or in literature. Indeed, the Independent Review of the Primary Curriculum [Department for Children, Schools and Families (DCSF) 2009] stressed the co-relationship of high levels of competence in written and spoken language and reading with exposure to stories and creative use of ICT. Further, a large body of research refers to the creative use of digital media within primary education that facilitates teaching of the codes and conventions through which moving images construct narratives and tell stories (Parker 2002; Swain 2003; Matthews-DeNatale 2008).

Loveless (2003) has suggested that the prescriptive curriculum, especially in relation to primary literacy and numeracy, together with the focus on testing, has limited primary teachers' ability to make spaces for creative activity, especially, that which insightfully utilizes multimedia within the classroom. Walker and Gleaves (2008) and Phelps and Maddison (2008) have suggested that the focus on iterative improvement, subject updating, all within a context of financial restraint within the secondary curriculum has fostered a belief among some teachers that creativity is simply the production and refinement of increasingly detailed and ornate work in whatever disciplinary context. Indeed, teachers' wider motivations to make creative ICT 'spaces' is questionable: studies repeatedly demonstrate that teachers from a wide range of disciplines appear to show marked contradictions between their self-reported beliefs about pupils' creativity in ICT and their actual pedagogic practices aimed at its development. Teachers' experiences, beliefs and perceptions of ICT-related creativity deserve much greater scrutiny, therefore, and it is these issues that will occupy the next section.

Teachers' practices in the creative ICT classroom

The foregoing discussion demonstrates the contested disciplinary and curricular basis of ICT and digital creativity. Studies attest to the fact that this confusion remains one of the major sites of pedagogic concern for teachers, including ICT teachers, in the twenty-first century (Devolder *et al.* 2010; Sang *et al.* 2010; Shaheen 2010), many of whom have limited familiarity and experience with digital media and technology, and yet are expected to fulfil demanding continual professional development commitments in order to equip them to create what BIS (2009) has termed 'digital Britons'. Yet despite this, the fact that ICT is seen by educationalists and teachers alike as both a means and a catalyst to innovate and improve education suggests that many teachers persist against all odds in introducing elements of creative themes and activities into their existing curricula. Individuals though, appear to play an equally significant role in creative ICT practices, whether through the vision and dynamism of ICT coordinators, basement musicians, inveterate bloggers, or addicted gamers obsessed with 'mods': the fact is, as Hammond *et al.* (2009) point out, exemplary use of ICTs that truly enrich the learner occurs through creative practices that are framed in ecological terms. Tan (2001: 51) calls these 'unconventional learning environments'. In the context of these 'unconventional learning environments', what particular activities and ideas might teachers do in order to both enrich the learner and begin to incorporate problem solving, creative cognition, and social interaction? The following chart (Table 7.1), drawing on research (Gyabak and Godina 2011; Potter 2006) into the use of digital media technologies (DMTs) and digital applications within the primary classroom, demonstrates some of the activities and applications that may be used to promote and facilitate creativity in primary ICT.

TABLE 7.1 Starting points for creativity and problem solving through ICT in the primary school

CREATIVITY ELEMENT	EXAMPLE OF ACTIVITY FOCUS	TYPE OF DIGITAL MEDIA TECHNOLOGY OR DIGITAL APPLICATION USED
Problem solving	– Developing forums for including diversity of ability and interest within the classroom – Carrying out research about different points of view on a global perspective	– Digital video and still cameras, iPhones – YouTube, Twitter – International News websites
Creative cognition	– Creating non-linear text, designing, scaling and formatting presentations for different effects, purposes and audiences – Translating tales from personal narratives to digital stories	– Interactive whiteboards, tablets – Prezi, Powerpoint, Wordle – Digital camera, flatbed scanner, microphone, music keyboard, few instruments, iMovie, Movie Maker, Garage Band

CREATIVITY ELEMENT	EXAMPLE OF ACTIVITY FOCUS	TYPE OF DIGITAL MEDIA TECHNOLOGY OR DIGITAL APPLICATION USED
Social interaction	– Enriching talking and listening experiences through vodcasts and podcasts for children, particularly with concentration difficulties and/or delayed language development – Promoting empathy and understanding through community feedback and support through film-making and/or performance videos	– iPods, mobile phones, iPads. – Audacity (PCs), Garage Band, Android and iOs for mobile phones – Ning, YouTube

So what is a 'creative' ICT teacher?

Although there is much evidence to support the importance of the role that teachers play in the development of learners' creative potential within these 'unconventional learning environments' in ICT, there is disagreement as to the exact nature of the pedagogic practices that facilitate it. At early years level, for example, the predominance of structured play and rudimentary experimentation as factors in the development of pupils' ICT-related creativity is well documented, and as a result, pedagogic practices that mirror such concepts tend to predominate (Kangas 2010). In contrast, at the primary level, modelling becomes an important precursor to pupils' emerging creative ability, teachers often tending to borrow social and cultural ICT capital and enlist children as co-constructors of meaning and creation (Wheeler et al. 2002; Rojas-Drummond et al. 2008; Graham 2009). Kampylis et al. (2009) assert that this is because primary teachers spend a considerable amount of time with their pupils, engaging in a diverse range of learning activities that not only communicate teachers' beliefs about creativity, but also give full rein to the 'complex expression of creative agency' (Kampylis et al. 2009: 15). At secondary level, individual teachers usually spend far less time with particular pupils, and during interactions, their conceptions of creativity are enacted and experienced by pupils as functions of explicit curriculum subjects and thus shaped by their disciplinary vocabularies of creative expression. But as Abbott et al. (2001) pointed out, and Hammond et al. (2009) more recently, this is both a saving grace and damning curse, the former because at least formal disciplines make potential space for subjects such as ICT that are in constant evolution, having permanently to renegotiate their curricular justification, the latter because such frequently straitjacketed curricula interpretations of creative ICT may well obscure the potential for unconventional responses to real-life problems.

Such contradictions are evident in teachers' practices: Kampylis et al. (2009) report in their study, for example, that despite a sample of Greek primary teachers almost uniformly agreeing that the pupils' creative potential must be developed across the curriculum, the majority felt that it could only be developed authentically within the 'creative' subjects of music, theatre and art. Shaheen's (2010) study of Pakistani teachers found that despite policy requirements to represent creativity 'holistically' and 'comprehensively', teachers were unsure of its disciplinary status and conceptual underpinnings, leaving pupils 'weaker in other areas such as being able to produce abstract titles, and remaining open to going beyond the "ordinary" in their thinking' (Shaheen 2010: 17). Hennessy *et al.* (2005) found in their research that, whilst many teachers say they are prioritizing creativity within the curriculum, any systematically planned opportunities to develop it evidently rest primarily upon disciplinary curricula concepts instead.

Making links to primary teachers' creative use of ICTs, one can draw immediate insights: Sang *et al.* (2010) illustrate that those teachers willing to integrate ICT into the curriculum are the ones who hold the strongest constructivist beliefs and are happy to work alongside children to further learning goals. This aspect of co-working is, of course, critical in creative ICT use. Many pupils, even at the earliest stages of formal education, are more ICT literate than their teachers. This finding is supported by Hermans *et al.* (2008: 1506) who pointed out in their study that, although the ICT use in classes of primary teachers could 'hardly be described as innovative in nature', the teachers using ICT most creatively had a combination of constructivist beliefs and prior experience in ICT that helped them to be confident, persistent and risk-taking.

These qualities of a 'creative' ICT teacher who is able to practise 'creative pedagogies' are critical: teaching in England currently stands at a crossroads in terms of the balance of subject knowledge and professional expectations. In addition, there are profound changes in the digital landscape, in relation to education, and the place of individuals within society. But as Slaouti and Barton (2007) and Phelps and Maddison (2008) point out, there is scarce research that addresses the origins of the personal and professional factors that impact on individual teachers' willingness to integrate ICT and new media into their classes, despite studies that repeatedly demonstrate that teachers' career narratives exert a very significant influence on their pedagogic thinking (Phelps and Maddison 2008; Hammond *et al.* 2009). The balance of teacher knowledge and professional knowledge is difficult and a source of continuing career-long reconciliation for many teachers. But amongst teachers in many disciplines, such as science, mathematics and language, there is a shared understanding of pedagogical and conceptual bases and themes. In contrast, as a result of the very wide professional and disciplinary basis of ICT (McBride 2008), many teachers have almost no commonality in philosophical approach or practical significance of their subject, a situation illustrated clearly in the many studies cited within this chapter.

Concluding thoughts

The integration of both ICT and digital literacy and creativity within the curriculum has become high priorities in UK maintained schools over the last decade, just as they have internationally. According to Van Damme (2009), the shifting uncertainty of twenty-first century society requires talented and creative people who do not simply respond to innovation, but generate it themselves, in other words, 'pedagogic entrepreneurs'. But, as this chapter has demonstrated, in the context of ICT, that is not enough. One must also be a digital pedagogic entrepreneur, with a high-level capability with ICT and digital media who can, in addition, fashion them creatively both reflecting social change and incorporating sophisticated 'texts' from informal contexts that are transferable to multiple real-life contexts.

But this chapter also illustrates the significant practical and philosophical gaps in reconciling pedagogic entrepreneurship in ICT and understanding how teachers arrive at their meanings of ICT and digital creativity. In many ways, there appears to be an ultimate irony about the place of creativity within ICT. As Bishop (2009: 48) points out, ICTs and digital creativity foster possibilities for teachers' 'self-authorings' in relation to their professional and pedagogical development, but these are potentially intimidating for some teachers because they overturn many teachers' conventional scripts of formally acquired knowledge within context-free settings. What is evident from the discussion however, is the widespread expectation that teachers will continue to foster and facilitate the ICT and digital creativity that has been rapidly integrated into most aspects of the school curriculum not just in the UK, but internationally. This chapter clearly points to the fact that creativity's basis in ICT needs to be considered as a function of personal agency much more fully and carefully.

References

Abbott, C., Lachs, V. and Williams, L. (2001) 'Fool's gold or hidden treasure: are computers stifling creativity?,' *Journal of Education Policy*, 16(5): 479–87.

Arnone, M., Reynolds, R. and Marshall, T. (2009) 'The effect of early adolescents' psychological needs satisfaction upon their perceived competence in information skills and intrinsic motivation for research', *School Libraries Worldwide*, 15(2): 115–34.

Banaji, S. and Burn, A. (2007) *The Rhetorics of Creativity: a review of the literature*, London: The Arts Council of England.

Banaji, S., Burn, A. and Buckingham, D. (2010) *The Rhetorics of Creativity: a literature review*, 2nd edn London: Creativity, Culture and Education.

Becker, G. (2000) 'The association of creativity and psychopathology: its cultural–historical origins', *Creativity Research Journal*, 13(1): 45–53.

BIS (2009) *Digital Britain: Final Report*, London: Department for Business Innovation and Skills.

Bishop, J. (2009) 'Pre-service teacher discourses: authoring selves through multimodal compositions', *Digital Culture and Education*, 1(1): 31–50.

Buckingham, D. (2007) *Children's Learning in an Age of Digital Culture*, Cambridge: Polity Press.

Calvani, A., Cartelli, A., Fini, A. and Ranieri, M. (2008) 'Models and Instruments for Assessing Digital Competence at School', *Journal of e-Learning and Knowledge Society*, 4(3): 183–93.

Carr, N. (2008) 'Is google making us stupid? What the internet is doing to our brains', *The Atlantic*, 302(1): 56–63.

Cooper, B. and Brna, P. (2002) 'Supporting high quality interaction and motivation in the classroom using ICT: the social and emotional learning and engagement in the NIMIS project', *Education, Communication and Information*, 2(1/2): 113–38.

Davies, T. (2006) 'Creative teaching and learning in Europe: promoting a new paradigm', *Curriculum Journal*, 17(1): 37–57.

Department for Children, Schools and Families (DCSF) (2009) *Independent Review of the Primary Curriculum (the Rose Review)*. Online. Available at http://www.education.gov.uk/publications/Primary_curriculum-report.pdf (accessed 19 January 2011).

Devolder, A., Vanderlinde, R., Van Braak, J. and Tondeur, J. (2010) 'Identifying multiple roles of ICT coordinators', *Computers and Education*, 55(4): 1651–5.

Drent, M. and Meelissen, M. (2008) 'Which factors obstruct or stimulate teacher educators to use ICT innovatively?', *Computers and Education*, 51(1): 187–99.

Fasko, D. (2001) 'Education and creativity', *Creativity Research Journal*, 13: 317–28.

Gardner, H. (1993) *Multiple Intelligences: The theory in practice*, New York: Basic Books.

Gomoluch, K. and Whittaker, G. (2007) *Developing a New Curriculum: 'chartered street' or 'valley wild'?* Paper presented at a conference organized by the University of Wales Institute, Cardiff, in collaboration with the Higher Education Academy, Cardiff: January 8–10.

Graham, L. (2009) 'It was a challenge but we did it! Digital worlds in a primary classroom', *Literacy*, 43(2): 107–14.

Gyabak, K. and Godina, H. (2011) 'Digital storytelling in Bhutan: A qualitative examination of new media tools used to bridge the digital divide in a rural community school', *Computers and Education*, 57(4): 2236–43.

Hammond, M., Crosson, S., Fragkouli, E., Ingram, J., Johnston-Wilder, P., Johnston-Wilder, S., Kingston, Y., Pope, M. and Wray, D. (2009) 'Why do some student teachers make very good use of ICT? An exploratory case study', *Technology, Pedagogy and Education*, 18(1): 59–73 (1747-5139).

Haydn, T. and Barton, R. (2007) 'Common needs and different agendas: How trainee teachers make progress in their ability to use ICT in subject teaching. Some lessons from the UK', *Computers and Education*, 49(4): 1018–36.

Hennessy, S. Ruthven, K. and Brindley, S. (2005) 'Teacher perspectives on integrating ICT into subject teaching: commitment, constraints, caution and change', *Journal of Curriculum Studies*, 37(2): 155–92.

Hermans, R., Tondeur, J., Van Braak, J. and Valcke, M. (2008) 'The impact of primary school teachers' educational beliefs on the classroom use of computers', *Computers and Education*, 51(3): 1499–509.

Hosgurur, V. and Bilasa, P. (2009) 'The problem of creative education in information society', *Procedia Social and Behavioral Sciences*, 1: 713–17.

Jimoyiannis, A. and Komis, V. (2007) 'Examining teacher's beliefs about ICT in education', *Teachers Development*, 11(2): 149–73.

Kampylis, P., Berki, E. and Saariluoma, P. (2009) 'In-service and prospective teachers' conceptions of creativity', *Thinking Skills and Creativity*, 4(1): 15–29.

Kangas, M. (2010) 'The school of the future: Theoretical and pedagogical approaches for creative and playful learning environments.' Unpublished doctoral dissertation, *Acta Universitatis Lapponiensis* 188, University of Lapland, Faculty of Education, Finland. Rovaniemi: University of Lapland Printing Centre.

Lai, K.W., Trewern, A. and Pratt, K. (2002) 'Computer coordinators as change agents: some New Zealand observations', *Journal of Technology and Teacher Education*, 10: 539–51.

Li, Y. and Ranieri, M. (2010) 'Are "digital natives" really digitally competent? A study on Chinese teenagers', *British Journal of Educational Technology*, 41(6).

Loveless, A. (2003) 'Creating spaces in the primary curriculum: ICT in creative subjects', *Curriculum Journal*, 14(1): 5–21.

Maslow, A.H. (1962) 'Lessons from the peak-experiences', *Journal of Humanistic Psychology*, 2: 9–18.

Matthews-DeNatale, G. (2008) *Digital Storytelling - tips and resources*. Online. Available at http://www.educause.edu/Resources/DigitalStoryMakingUnderstandin/162538 (accessed 16 March 2009).

McBride, N. (2008) *The State of A Level Computing*: comment piece for the Chartered Institute for IT. Online. Available at http://www.bcs.org/ (accessed 2 March 2011).

Nicholls, J.G. (1972) 'Creativity in the person who will never produce anything original and useful: the concept of creativity as a normally distributed trait', *American Psychologist*, 27: 717–27.

Odena, O. and Welch, G. (2009) 'A generative model of teachers' thinking on musical creativity', *Psychology of Music*, 37(4): 416–42.

Oliver, R. (1993) 'The influence of training on beginning teachers' use of computers', *Australian Educational Computing*, July: 189–96.

Parker, D. (2002) 'Show us a story: an overview of recent research and resource development work at the British Film Institute', *English in Education*, 36(1): 38–44.

Pearson, M. and Naylor, S. (2006) 'Changing contexts: teacher professional development and ICT pedagogy', *Education and Information Technologies*, 11(3–4): 283–91.

Phelps, R. and Maddison, C. (2008) 'ICT in the secondary visual arts classroom: a study of teachers' values, attitudes and beliefs', *Australasian Journal of Educational Technology*, 24(1): 1–14.

Plomp, T. and Pelgrum, W.J. (1991) 'Introduction of computers in education: State of the art in eight countries', *Computers and Education*, 17(3): 249–58.

Potter, J. (2006) 'Carnival visions: digital creativity in teacher education', *Learning, Media and Technology*, 31(1): 51–66.

Rojas-Drummond, S.M. Albarrán, D. and Littleton, K. (2008) 'Collaboration, creativity and the co-construction of oral and written texts mediated by ICT', Thinking Skills and Creativity – Special Issue, in K. Littleton, S. Rojas-Drummond and D. Miell (eds), *Creative Collaborations: Socio-Cultural Perspectives*, 3(3): 177–91.

Sak, U. (2004) 'About creativity, giftedness, and teaching the creatively gifted in the classroom', *Roeper Review*, 26: 216–22.

Sang, G., Valcke, M., Tondeur, J. and van Braak, J. (2010) 'Student teachers' thinking processes and ICT integration: predictors of prospective teaching behaviors with educational technology', *Computers and Education*, 54(1): 103–12.

Sanz, A. and Romero, D. (2007) *Literatures in the Digital Era: theory and praxis*, Cambridge: Cambridge Scholars Publishing.

Scholtz, A. and Livingstone, D.W. (2005) *Knowledge workers and the 'new economy' in Canada: 1983–2004*. Paper presented at the 3rd annual WALL conference, 19 June.

Sefton-Green, J. and Sinker, R. (eds) (2000) *Evaluating Creativity: making and learning by young people*, London: Routledge.

Selwyn, N. and Bullon, K. (2000) 'Primary children's use of ICT', *British Journal of Educational Technology*, 31(4): 321–32.

Shaheen, R. (2010) *An investigation into the factors enhancing or inhibiting primary school children's creativity in Pakistan*. Unpublished Ph.D. thesis, University of Birmingham.

Simge, E. (2010) 'Creativity in the early years of education'. Paper presented at the *Early Years Conference 2010, The Rights of the Child, Vancouver, B.C., Canada*, 4–6 February 2010.

Slaouti, D. and Barton, A. (2007) 'Opportunities for practice and development: newly qualified teachers and the use of ICT in teaching foreign languages in English secondary school contexts', *Journal of In-service Education*, 3(4): 405–24.

Stern, S. (2008) 'Producing sites, exploring identities: youth online authorship', in D. Buckingham (ed.) *Youth, Identity, and Digital Media*, Cambridge, MA: MIT Press, pp. 95–118.

Swain, C. (2003) 'Using digital video to study history', *Social Education*, 67(3): 154–7.

Taddei, F. (2009) *Training Creative and Collaborative Knowledge-Builders: a major challenge for 21st century education*, Report of the OECD, Paris: OECD.

Tan, A.G. (2001) 'Singaporean teachers' perception of activities useful for fostering creativity', *Journal of Creative Behavior*, 35: 131–48.

Turvey, K. (2006) 'Towards deeper learning through creativity within online communities in primary education', *Computers and Education*, 47(2): 309–21.

United Nations Educational, Scientific and Cultural Organization (UNESCO) (2005) *ICT in Schools: a handbook for teachers, or how ICT can create new, open learning environments*, UNESCO Division of Higher Education. Paris: UNESCO.

Van Damme, D. (2009) *Beyond Chalk and Talk: creativity in the classroom*, Brussels: European Policy Centre, EU, 30 March.

Walker, C. and Gleaves, A. (2008) 'Creativity in education: an exploration of students' perceptions and experiences in higher education', *Irish Educational Studies*, 27(1): 41–54.

Ward, T.B., Smith, S.M., and Finke, R.A. (1999) 'Creative cognition', in R.J. Sternberg (ed.) *Handbook of Creativity*, New York: Cambridge University Press, pp. 189–212.

Wheeler, S., Waite S. and Bromfield, C. (2002) 'Promoting creativity through the use of ICT', *Journal of Computer Assisted Learning*, 18(3): 367–78.

8

Recognizing Creativity

Douglas Newton

What is being recognized?

People are different and that means some show themselves to be generally more creative than others for a variety of reasons, including genes, past opportunities, practice, and the response of others to their creative activity. Psychologists, like Torrance (1974) and Alenizi (2008), are often interested in ways of identifying such people. For instance, when asked to list as many uses for a paperclip as they can, some people seem to have very fertile imaginations. They show it again when asked to think of how two, supposedly incongruent objects like, say, a paperweight and a dictionary, are similar. Evidence of divergent thinking like this is taken to indicate those with a ready, general, creative ability. For some purposes, this is useful but not necessarily for a teacher teaching a specific topic in a specific subject to a specific class using specific resources. Having lots of ideas is not always what counts when it comes to being creative or solving a problem in a specific context. Suppose, for instance, your car breaks down and you need to get home; you might use a pogo-stick, hang from the legs of a large bird, or swing from branch to branch through the trees. These may be imaginative suggestions but are they generally not feasible ways of getting home. What you need is an idea suitably constrained by the situation: imagination alone is not enough.

Others are interested in the influence of a particular approach or teaching resource on some aspects of creative behaviour. Holbrook *et al.* (2003), for instance, demonstrated that including social issues in science teaching tended to increase students' asking of questions and causal suggestions. Useful as this is, it still leaves teachers without much to guide their day-to-day support for each learner. Ellis and Lawrence (2009) similarly describe assessment to gauge the impact of a creative, arts-based curriculum on children's achievement. They add, however, that the assessment made teachers more aware of and reflective about learning so that they could 'fine-tune their practice to support individual learners'. This is the aim of the discussion in this chapter. It is not about identifying people who are generally creative or uncreative, or even about identifying those who are creative in a particular subject. Instead, it focuses on finding clues which could help a teacher foster a child's creativity in a given activity and in subsequent activities. Assessment for learning is a popular expression but, here, it might more usefully be described as 'assessment for teaching' as its primary purpose is to inform the teacher so that individual children's needs may be met.

Is evaluating creativity a good thing?

Any desire to assess creativity is anathema to some people. They argue that there is something special, ineffable or mystical about creativity and attempts to assess it only sully, demean and insult it, squeezing out its essence and reducing it to the mundane. Others argue that it is impossible to assess creativity because the range of creative responses is essentially infinite – a mark scheme is impossible (see e.g. Rogers and Fasciato 2005; de la Harpe and Peterson 2008). Others argue that, creativity is a private matter and not for others to judge (Sefton-Green 2000). In the classroom, some believe attempts to assess creativity risk damaging the child's inclination to be creative, explore possible worlds and sometimes blamelessly fail in the attempt. In effect, the child would learn to avoid thought and action which produce low grades. Others see it as one aspect of experience still free from the tyranny of examination, a welcome relief for the child in a world of measuring, tagging and labelling. Some are concerned that, in a system obsessed with 'performativity', it becomes another mechanistic assessment which tells us little about the child and only serves to find teachers and schools wanting (Burnard and White 2008).

Reading these concerns again, I find I could agree with most of them. However, a step back is needed. Sefton-Green (2000) considered words of overlapping meaning, like assessment and evaluation, in relation to creative activity. For some, assessment has connotations of quantitative, right–wrong judgements of children in order to label them. Their nervousness seems to stem, at least in part, from the formal, mechanistic, quantitative connotations of assessment which could ride roughshod over the unpressured nature of creative activity or intrude upon the few classroom activities seen as free of assessment. The aim here, however, is to look for clues to inform the process of teaching. This seems to be better served by a thoughtful engagement with what the child does and produces; see, for example, Ellis and Lawrence's (2009) account of the Creative Learning Assessment project to assess creative activity in the arts. The word *evaluation* tends to be associated with qualitative, qualified appraisals, although it can include quantity. *Recognizing* and *evaluating* creative thought and action seem to capture something of what is needed. If creative activity is to be more than a pastime, some form of evaluation is inevitable if the teacher is to help the child think and act more productively. Some scepticism, however, stems from the infinite variety of creative products which could be generated by a given task. How can a teacher's mark scheme allow for that variety? This supposed obstacle is a red herring as what is of interest to the teacher is how the child arrived at the product. Fostering creativity is about helping the child acquire thought and action associated with successful creative activity and also developing a disposition to use these unprompted. There has been some debate about what exactly should be assessed. Fox (1963) and Rust (2002) argue that there is nothing unique about the creative process and attention should be on attributes of the product; others believe it should be the process (e.g. Treffinger and

Poggio 1972; Houtz and Krug 1995). In practice, anything which gives teachers clues about the child's activity and disposition, mental or otherwise, could help them help the child do it better. Clues might come from interaction with children as they work (the process in action) *and* from examining what the children create (the product of the action) and there can be a strong correlation between assessments of the creative process and assessments of the creative product (Hennessey 1994). If there happens to be 30 different products, that does not impede their evaluation. In theory, each product could help a teacher to tailor the child's learning experience. In practice, commonalities are likely to make the task of personalized provision less onerous. Taken together, an unobtrusive evaluation of children's creative activity need not degrade the activity's qualities. As a more or less everyday need, fostering creativity has value and deserves to be cultivated in an informed way. Evaluation can provide that information.

How can creativity be evaluated?

Evaluation has little to do with giving a product a mark out of ten. Clues to thinking are needed and there are two sources: the first is in the doing of the task, the thought and action in it, the process; the second is from the outcome, the result, the product. The first calls for observation and interaction with the children while they work; the second can be a more leisurely inspection of the outcome of that work, perhaps with some clarification from the children.

Clues from the process

What should we look for in the doing of the task? The Qualifications and Curriculum Authority (QCA) (2004) points out that the questions children ask can provide clues to their thinking. But simply asking questions and even being curious is not enough: the kind of question matters. For instance, 'What time is it, Miss?' is readily satisfied with a glance at the clock. On the other hand, 'How can I find the time if I don't have a clock?' has more promise. The child could, of course, be directed to a bumper 'How To' book and construct a sundial according to its instructions. On the other hand, reflecting the question back may make the child puzzle over the problem and, perhaps with some guidance, produce a different solution. Children's questions can indicate a state of mind which is set to speculate, consider possibilities, try ideas and produce solutions; all it needs is a nudge from the teacher to start the wheels turning. A child with a disposition to be creative may not even need that nudge. Ideas, however, do not come out of nothing and observation will show what children do with the question, how they clarify it, how they draw on prior knowledge, how they fertilize it with new ideas, how they use resources which help them think and visualize their ideas, what they do with possibilities and blind alleys, how they sketch out and try ideas, how they reflect on the developing product, and whether they act upon those reflections. Strengths and weaknesses may show themselves in any of these and the teacher may intervene to guide, suggest, point out and otherwise develop ways of thinking and working which support the creative process and do not eliminate it. As the teacher moves from child to child, common patterns of need may become apparent and the teacher may plan other events to address those needs or consolidate good practices. Some things to look for in creative thought and action are listed in Table 8.1, but consider these within the limits of children's experiences and ability. You may wish to add others.

TABLE 8.1 Some evaluation clues (processes)

CHILDREN WORKING WITH	BEHAVIOURS
Creative seeds	Asking questions, showing curiosity, responding to these, clarifying the task, simplifying the task.
The child's ideas	Using prior knowledge, adding to their knowledge, exploring the potential of resources, using strategies (e.g. pencil and paper) to support thinking and communicate ideas, thinking of possibilities, making suggestions, keeping an open mind, suspending judgement, toying with ideas, experimenting, changing the approach from an unproductive one.
Suitable ideas	Reflecting on constraints, practicality, feasibility, difficulties, fitness for purpose, appropriateness, plausibility; acting on the reflections, explores options.
The product's quality	Reflecting on the quality of the developing product, considering aesthetics, acting on those reflections.
The product's acceptability	When relevant, taking into account the need for consideration for others, human and animal rights, moral and ethical matters, school rules and the law.
The child's tendencies	Inclination to find out and do unprompted, self-reliance, persistence, willingness to collaborate when needed, able to work flexibly.

Some examples from the process

English

In English, the teacher read Helen Cowcher's *Rainforest* (1990, Farrar, Straus and Giroux, New York) to her class of six-year-olds. This is an illustrated story of the threat to the habitat of the animals of the rainforest, seen through the eyes of some of the animals. The children expressed their feelings about the animals' plight and the people causing it. One of the animals not mentioned in the story was the orang-utan. The teacher showed them Ollie, a large, stuffed toy version of an orang-utan and had him 'tell' the children that he, too, lived in the rainforest. During the day, Ollie told them, he eats leaves and berries and each night he makes a bed of leaves and branches in the tree tops. Now, he is very worried. 'Ollie wasn't in this story', the teacher said. 'What if he had been, what would he have told us?' She paused while they thought about it. 'What if *you* were Ollie, what would *you* tell everyone?' The children made suggestions and the teacher encouraged them to pick up and develop each other's ideas. 'What if Ollie could write?' she asked, 'Could he write a letter and complain?' They agreed and suggested people to write to. The teacher pointed out that Ollie could not write so they would have to be him and do it for him. 'But what could we say?' she asked. She generalized it to telling about why he was worried, telling about how he felt, and telling about what needed to be done. She had prepared some sheets of coloured paper cut like a silhouette of Ollie for the letter-writing and the children were soon engrossed in the task. Occasionally, they asked, 'Can I ...?' but if this required a decision about the content of the letter, the teacher told the children they could decide what Ollie wanted to say themselves. Some of them were a little uneasy about this freedom and sought reassurance. Others seized the opportunity. The mechanics of writing distracted some from the object of the task so the teacher circulated amongst the class, reminding them of the goal and encouraging persistence. The children wanted envelopes for their letters so these were provided and names written on them.

The teacher felt that the task had exercised several aspects of the creative process. The children had the opportunity to choose and construct sentences to communicate thoughts and elicit sympathy and help. Some had shown an embryonic form of a concern for quality with a desire to improve what they had written. The nervousness of some about taking decisions was noted; further opportunities would be provided to overcome the reluctance. Although the children had shown interest and curiosity and asked pertinent questions, the teacher wished she had let them choose an animal themselves as this may have increased interest, engagement, imagination and persistence.

Design and technology

In design and technology, some eight-year-old children made a simple, wooden crocodile, following instructions. The teacher then pointed out that their crocodiles did not have tails and set the task of designing, making and fitting a tail to their crocodiles which could bend and flick like the real thing. Various materials were available and the children explored their properties then returned to their tables to generate and develop ideas. The teacher noted that a few of the children simply picked up materials, looked at them, and returned them to the box. She suspected that they were simply considering appearances and not physical properties, a concern which was confirmed when these children made little progress and were inclined to give up. She collected them around the box of materials and picked up a strip of felt. 'Would this do', she asked. 'It's the wrong colour', one boy said. 'What about this?' she asked, picking up a length of brown and green wool. 'It doesn't look right. It's too thin', they said doubtfully. Satisfied that her suspicion was well-founded, she went back to the starting point, eliciting from them that the first need was for a flexible material, putting aside appearances for the moment. She pretended to think it through with them and they sorted the materials into two piles of 'bendy' and 'not bendy', then selected from the first those which they thought might make a tail. With her help, they identified the next hurdle: how to make the bendy material look more like a crocodile's tail. Each took the material of their choice but the teacher paired them and told them to help each other decide how to make realistic tails. The teacher now gave some time to the others but planned to return to help them identify and talk about the next problem: attaching the tails to their models.

The teacher decided that a serious source of difficulty was these children's superficial engagement with the materials and their premature closing down of possibilities. She modelled with them the process of breaking down the problem into its parts, the first of which was to choose a material with potential. She also set them up for the second part, namely, making the material more crocodile-like, and prepared herself for possibly helping with the final part, namely, attaching the tail. She also made a mental note that she would give more attention to practising the breaking of a problem into its parts in subsequent activities.

Music

In music, children may be asked to create a melody with the aid of a computer (see e.g. Hewitt 2008). Some nine-year-olds were shown how to use the programme. 'It's like what you get on an ice-cream van', suggested one girl. 'Can we do that? Can we make an ice-cream tune?' asked another. 'Can you?' asked the teacher. The children believed they could and there was some oral rehearsal of the small number of van melodies they knew. The teacher had them explore the characteristics of such jingles and various attributes were listed, including 'loud', 'happy', 'jangly', 'short', 'easy to remember'. The children took turns to construct their tunes, building sequences of notes and adjusting them to produce the effect they wanted. At times, she could hear children ask, 'How did you make it do that?' They would then experiment and use or abandon the idea. During this time, the teacher talked with the children, asking them about the effects they wanted and how they were achieving them. Generally, the children repeatedly played back their developing melodies, listening to them carefully and adjusting them until they 'liked' them and they were 'finished'. When needed, the teacher reminded them of the attributes they sought and that others had to like the tune, too. One child wanted his tune to be 'really loud' so that everyone in the street would know the van was there. 'Oh, dear!' said the teacher. 'Poor Mr Brown's on night shift and is in bed, asleep'. The boy suggested that the van driver could turn the volume down near Mr Brown's house. Another child was indignant about it. 'Don't be silly! How will he know who's in bed!' she said. He decided to reduce the volume himself. The class listened to their melodies in turn and felt they had achieved their goal.

The teacher felt some satisfaction with the activity. Her plan had been for the children to construct a melody for a door bell, telephone or birthday greeting but the children's request had proved fruitful. The characteristics of what they were to produce had come from the children and they had largely worked to them, producing 'fit-for-purpose' products which the children themselves found to be pleasing. The teacher was particularly gratified by one child's comment: 'I like mine and it's different.'

Clues from the product

People who know a subject or activity well can agree to a remarkable extent about which products are more creative than others. In what Amabile (1983a, 1983b, 1996) has called 'consensual assessment', such experts simply rate the products intuitively according to what creativity means to them. The order in which they place the products is usually very similar. In the classroom, Hennessey (1994) studied teachers' intuitive, holistic assessment of elementary school children's storytelling. They, too, tended to agree with one another. Hickey (2001) did something very similar to rate the musical compositions of nine- and ten-year-olds. Again, there was a high level of agreement. Cropley (2001) concluded that gauging creativity intuitively, that is, without conscious reasoning (Colman 2003) and largely using the 'undermind' (Claxton 1997), is not as difficult as expected. Accordingly, we might expect a teacher to be able to identify strengths and weaknesses in a child's product and make inferences about the thought and action that produced them. This optimism, however, has its limits.

First, it assumes that the teacher knows the subject well. A test by Newton (2010) revealed a very low level of agreement amongst primary school teachers assessing children's created scientific explanations. Such teachers must teach a wide range of subjects and they cannot be expected to be experts in all of them. Some of their difficulty came from explanations which were very imaginative but highly implausible. Unbridled imagination was often highly valued.

Second, there is the assumption that the teacher also knows what a creative product is from the point of view of the child, that is, what is novel and appropriate in the eyes of the children. Teachers comment on how difficult it is to judge something from a child's point of view. Hickey (2001) tried to overcome this by using children as judges of the musical compositions. Although this can work with older learners (Beattie 2000), the 7- and 12-year-old judges used by Hickey could not discriminate between liking and creativity. However, careful attention to the meaning of scientific creativity during teacher training showed itself able to improve the agreement of primary school teachers about creative products in science (Newton 2010). Furthermore, their ratings tended to reflect the definitions of creativity provided by bodies like the NACCCE (National Advisory Committee on Creative and Cultural Education; see Chapter 1).

This suggests that teachers can, to some extent, recognize creative work when they see it. They are generally better at it if they have had more experience of the subject and of the norms of children's creative performance in that subject and with training and help. A teacher, knowing his or her limits, may also be able to seek assistance from a willing colleague with appropriate experience and expertise. But what useful information can such an appraisal of the product tell the teacher? Various attributes may be considered, according to what the task has to offer and the age, experience and abilities of the children. The list in Table 8.2 relates to the product, and points to some things to consider. Again, you may wish to add others.

Some examples from the product

Mathematics

In *mathematics*, Worthington and Carruthers (2003) describe a boy aged 5 years 6 months whose solution to the problem of finding out if the number 8 can be divided equally without a remainder. His solution was a depiction of two of what he called 'tweedle birds'. Eight eggs were shared between them so that each had four. The final conclusion

TABLE 8.2 Some evaluation clues (products)

ATTRIBUTE OF THE PRODUCT	ASK YOURSELF
Precursors	Does the product relate to the task? Did the child understand the task sufficiently? Was it intentional?
Novelty	Is the product purely reproductive? Is it a copy of someone else's product? What distinctive features does it have? Does it show imagination, novelty or originality for such children? Does it bring things together in an effective way for such children?
Appropriateness	Is the product believable, plausible, appropriate, fit-for-purpose, suitable according to what is expected in that domain, allowing for the children's age, experience and ability? Is it too far-fetched for such a child to believe?
Elegance	Is there evidence that the child attempted to produce a product of quality? To what extent was this successful, allowing for the age, experience and ability of the child? If it was not successful, why not?
Ethics/morality	If it was relevant to the task, to what extent could the child have taken into account the product's acceptability to others? Did the child do so? If not, what is needed?
General	Is there evidence of persistence or of other useful traits in the product? Does the product confirm or contradict the views you formed when interacting with the children while they worked?

was that the number could, indeed, be shared equally without anything left over, which he indicated by a tick placed next to the figure 8. The product here is a way of checking numbers to see if they are divisible by two without remainder. This is something which is in the child's head. The drawing and his explanation of it, taken together, allowed the teacher to grasp the child's invention. They offered evidence that the child had understood the task and created a procedure that is fit-for-purpose. The general idea is not novel to the world at large but it was novel to the child. It also has some elegance about it in that it is an economical and effective way of testing small numbers for division by two by a young child. In addition, the drawing showed that, to begin with, he had decided that the number could not be divided equally but he persisted in repeating his procedure and correcting his conclusion. The creative thought shown by this child is commendable. Future activities would probably reveal more about the child's thinking.

Science

In science, the teacher showed some nine-year-olds pictures of the Moon's surface. The children examined the pictures and agreed that the ground looked dry and dusty.

They also agreed that nobody lived there. His final picture was of craters. First, he asked the children to tell him what the circles were, then to explain how they were made and, finally, why we don't see lots of craters like these on the Earth. With the questions on the board as an *aide memoire*, the children thought about it, wrote their ideas and read them out to the class. One child said they were giant's boot prints and there are none on the Earth because there are no giants on the Earth. Another thought they were hollows left behind when big pools of water dried up and we don't have them on the Earth because the water hasn't dried up yet. Although these explanations were presented in the lesson, they are created products and could be evaluated as such. For instance, the teacher could be satisfied that these children attempted to solve the problem as posed and showed some imaginative thought, although the first child's account of giant's boot prints suggested that there might be a lack of critical thought appropriate to the context. The teacher smiled and said, 'That would make a good story. We might make up a story like that later. But are there *really* giants on the Moon?' The child agreed that there were not and the child said she really thought the 'pools of water' idea was the best one. The teacher felt that it was very plausible, given the age and experience of the children, and noted that some of the patches on the Moon were once thought to be seas. He was a little disappointed that some children had failed to produce something which amounted to an explanation. He decided that the next time he asked for an explanation in science, he would model the process, highlight the need for scientific plausibility in this context, have them work in small groups with access to a large sheet of paper and pencils, and he would move amongst them to encourage persistence. He was also as good as his word and returned to the giant's boot prints later in a story-building session, describing, in appropriate terms, the extent to which they could bend reality – '*What if* there really were giants on the Moon?'

Art

In *art*, some ten-year-old children were asked to paint pictures of themselves for display in the classroom. Each picture was to tell a visitor something more than the appearance of the child. One boy's picture showed him standing in a field, surrounded by grass dotted with flowers. He was depicted with his arms by his side, quite inanimate and with just the hint of a smile. 'I'm a peaceful sort of person', he said. 'It shows what I'm like', and it did (Hall and Thompson 2005). He had grasped the task and his picture had a calm, tranquillity about it coming from his choice of location, the objects in it and in his decision about the posture. Sternberg (2006) described creativity as being about decisions and there is evidence that they had been successfully taken here, conscious or otherwise. Of course, the picture would never find itself amongst great works of art but, allowing for the child's age, ability and experience, he had grasped the task, interpreted it appropriately, thought about himself, chosen what he would do, developed it appropriately and brought together a picture which reflected care for its quality. There were no concerns about consideration, ethics or morality, and the product alone was insufficient to provide direct evidence of persistence, other than in its completion. On this occasion, a teacher would probably be happy with an outcome like this and would tell the child that.

These examples do not, of course, exhaust all possibilities, even within one subject. For example, in English, children may construct a metaphor or give their interpretation of a short poem while in Science, they may construct an analogy or an experiment to test an idea, or, in History, they may be given some details of life in the trenches in the First World War then write some entries in a soldier's diary. But in all of these, the process and the product both can provide useful information for the teacher. This helps the teacher shape a lesson and it informs plans for subsequent lessons. Teachers might, for instance, ask themselves:

- Did the children grasp the problem? Did they explore it, identify its parameters or constraints and break it into sub-tasks? Do I need to spend some time on this aspect?

- Did the children produce ideas? If not, how did they deal with it? Do they recognize a blind alley? Do they need to acquire one or two strategies which might help get out of a blind alley? Do they explore what the resources offer? Can they withhold criticism or suspend disbelief appropriately? Can they develop an idea? What can I do to help?

- Do the children work within the constraints of the task and produce something appropriate or otherwise fit-for-purpose? Do they recognize the nature of the subject or endeavour and how this determines what counts, given their abilities and prior experiences? How can I help them grasp that not just anything goes?

- Do the children recognize that quality counts? Given that there is a feasible, appropriate idea, do they take care to craft the product? Would it help if I had the class examine some commercial products and discuss this aspect of them?

- Do the children consider others in their work? Do they act appropriately on those deliberations, allowing for their age and experience of the world? How can I highlight the need for this?

- Are the children persistent? Do they give up too easily? Do they try to create solutions to their own problems, given their limits and the situation? What can I do to inculcate useful dispositions?

Such thoughts should lead to lessons which try to add to the children's capabilities, rather than simply exercise the same capabilities or reinforce unwanted habits of thought and action. Children, however, are variable and because something is achieved in one context does not mean it will be achieved in another. Furthermore, no-one should assume that one creative activity in one subject can tell all. One creative activity is unlikely to provide the same opportunities as another; for instance, many do not offer opportunities for considering other people. And, of course, predispositions and habits of thought and action take time to establish.

Some cautionary notes

It is important to note that, although we may talk of novel, appropriate and elegant activity in all subjects, what novelty, appropriateness and elegance mean in one subject may not be quite the same as in another. A teacher needs to know this and adjust his or her thinking to suit the context. So, for instance, what could make a child's story of the orang-utan appropriately creative in English could be, amongst other things, the words chosen for the animal to speak in order to elicit the listeners' understanding and sympathy for its plight (see, for instance, Robinson and Ellis 2000). In science, the same child's constructed explanation of habitat loss would have to meet an expectation of regard for the realities of nature – the orang-utan cannot, after all, speak English – and avoid unnecessary complexity (Carey 2010), always allowing, of course, for the age and experience of the child concerned. While there is always a need to respect such differences, the danger may be at its greatest when the children are engaged in cross-curricular activity. Cross-curricular work can help children integrate their learning and make it more memorable and durable, but the teacher has to be clear what is to count as creative thought and action in each part of it. Teachers also need to bear in mind that creativity does not lie entirely in the product – the poem, the melody, the picture – but is also in what the reader, listener, observer perceives in it and thinks about it. Finally, being creative involves exercising a kind of freedom. How this is viewed can depend on the culture.

References

Alenizi, M. (2008) *Assessment of Creativity in Education*. Available at: http://www.coe.uga.edu/~gclinton/enclaves/images/systemscreativity.jpg (accessed 10 November 2010).

Amabile, T.M. (1983a) *The Social Psychology of Creativity*, New York: Springer-Verlag.

Amabile, T.M. (1983b) 'The social psychology of creativity: a componential conceptualization', *Journal of Personality and Social Psychology*, 45(2): 357–76.

Amabile, T.M. (1996) *Creativity in Context*, Boulder: Westview Press.

Beattie, D.K. (2000) 'Creativity in art: The feasibility of assessing current conceptions in the school context', *Assessment in Education: Principles, Policy and Practice*, 7(2): 175–92.

Burnard, P. and White, J. (2008) 'Creativity and performativity: counterpoints in British and Australian education', *British Educational Research Journal*, 34(5): 667–82.

Carey, T.V. (2010) 'Parsimony', *Philosophy Now*, 81: 6–8.

Claxton, G. (1997) *Hare Brain, Tortoise Mind*, London: Fourth Estate.

Colman, A.M. (2003) *A Dictionary of Psychology*, Oxford: Oxford University Press.

Cropley, A.J. (2001) *Creativity in Education and Learning*, London: RoutledgeFalmer.

de la Harpe, B. and Peterson, J.F. (2008) 'A model for holistic studio assessment in the creative disciplines', in the *Proceedings of the 2008 ATN Assessment Conference, Adelaide, Australia*.

Ellis, S. and Lawrence, B. (2009) 'The influence of the Creative Learning Assessment (CLA) on children's learning and teachers' teaching', *Literacy*, 43(1): 3–10.

Fox, H. (1963) 'A critique on creativity in science', in M. Coler (ed.) *Essays on Creativity in the Sciences*, New York: New York University Press, pp. 123–52.

Hall, C. and Thompson, P. (2005) 'Creative tensions? Creativity and basic skills in recent educational policy', *English in Education*, 39(3): 5–18.

Hennessey, B.A. (1994) 'The consensual assessment technique: An examination of the relationship between ratings of product and process creativity', *Creativity Research Journal*, 7(2): 193–208.

Hewitt, A. (2008) 'Children's creative collaboration during a computer-based music task', *International Journal of Educational Research*, 47: 11–26.

Hickey, M. (2001) 'An application of Amabile's consensual assessment technique for rating the creativity of children's musical composition', *Journal of Research in Music Education*, 49(3): 234–44.

Holbrook, J., Lains, A. and Rannikmäe, M. (2003) *The Influence of Social Issue-Based Science Learning Materials on Students' Learning*. Available at: http://www.ut.ee/eLSEEConf/Kogumik/Laius.pdf (accessed 11 November 2010).

Houtz, J.C., and Krug, D. (1995) 'Assessment of creativity', *Educational Psychology Review*, 7(3): 269–300.

Newton, D.P. (2010) 'Assessing the creativity of scientific explanations in elementary science: an insider-outsider view of intuitive assessment in the hypothesis space', *Research in Science and Technological Education*, 28(3): 187–201.

Qualifications and Curriculum Authority (QCA) (2004) *Creativity: find it, promote it.* London: QCA.

Robinson, M. and Ellis, V. (2000) 'Writing in English and responding in writing', in J. Sefton-Green and R. Sinker (eds) *Evaluating Creativity*, London: Routledge, pp. 70–88.

Rogers, M. and Fasciato, M. (2005) 'Can creativity be assessed?' Paper presented at the *British Educational Research Association Conference, University of Glamorgan, 14–17 September*.

Rust, C. (2002) 'The impact of assessment on student learning', *Active Learning in Higher Education*, 3: 145–57.

Sefton-Green, J. (2000) 'Introduction', in J. Sefton-Green and R. Sinker (eds) *Evaluating Creativity*, London: Routledge, pp. 1–15.

Sternberg, R.J. (2006) 'The nature of creativity', *Creativity Research Journal*, 18(1): 87–98.

Torrance, E.E. (1974) *Torrance Tests of Creative Thinking*, New Jersey: Princeton.

Treffinger, D. and Poggio, J. (1972) 'Needed research on the measurement of creativity', *Journal of Creative Behavior*, 8: 101–6.

Worthington, M. and Carruthers, E. (2003) 'Research uncovers children's creative mathematical thinking', *Primary Mathematics*, 7(3): 21–5.

9

'Creativity is Our Hope': A Wider Perspective on Creativity

Sophie Ward and Lynn Newton

Introduction

In 2006, the United Nations Educational, Scientific and Cultural Organization (UNESCO) held its first World Conference on Arts Education in Lisbon, Portugal, entitled *Building Creative Competencies for the 21st Century*. The conference, which was attended by 1200 participants from 97 member states, reported the findings from four preparatory Regional Conferences held in 2005 (for delegates from Asia and the Eastern Pacific; the Caribbean; Latin America; and Europe and North America) and also presented two national case studies on Mali and Oman. The UNESCO conference concluded with a report based on an international expert meeting, held in Australia in 2005 (UNESCO 2006: 4). The UNESCO conference was, then, truly global in its participants and also in its message, and the Director-General's proclamation that 'Creativity is our hope' captured the urgency of the conference proceedings (UNESCO 2006: 5). But why, we might ask, had the international community come to place such a high value on creativity? The answer to this question may be found in the conference *Working Document* (UNESCO 2006). Here, the four regional reports from their diverse, multicultural nations identify common tensions between cultural identity and economic and social well-being at the dawn of the twenty-first century.

In Asia and the Pacific Rim countries, one of the challenges is the 'need for imagination, creativity and collaboration as societies become more knowledge-based' (UNESCO 2006: 13). Caribbean 'societies-in-crisis' are compared with the Gordian knot, since problems have been frequently identifies but 'have not been solved' (UNESCO 2006: 19). In Latin America countries, where diversity was, until recently, perceived of as a weakness, the result was a reduction in 'learning and knowledge to particular cultural values and traditions' (UNESCO 2006: 22). Finally, in a changing Europe and North America, 'identity, society and culture [require] new types of teaching and learning ... focused on fostering cultural identity, creativity and social cohesion' (UNESCO 2006: 29, 39).

The concerns expressed by the authors of the *Working Document* not only reflect the widespread recognition that 'knowledge-based production' has overtaken traditional industries in wealth creation across the world (Pagano 2007: 662) but also an anxiety over the threat posed to cultural identity by this globalization. As noted by Dupas (2001: 1), 'global economic processes involve conflict and exclusion, especially in poor countries'. The worldwide increase in labour force mobility has resulted in the exploitation and vilification of economic migrants from poorer nations who are seen as taking jobs from local communities in more prosperous regions (Taran and Geronimi 2002) and as a disruption to the indigenous cultures. Furthermore, with globalization, convergence towards a single model of capitalism has been accompanied by pressure to abandon national cultures in favour of a global culture. According to Pagano (2007: 650), 'Differential access to world culture can become a traumatic division in a culturally convergent world', something touched upon frequently in the UNESCO's regional reports.

The authors of the *Working Document* were no doubt aware of the turbulence of the preceding century, in which millions of people have died in conflicts born of racial and cultural intolerance. It is perhaps logical to attempt to avoid the racial and cultural clashes that have plagued this recent history by cultivating a global culture to underpin the common financial market. Yet, while the authors of the *Working Document* do not challenge the principle of globalization, they do appear to take issue with an assumption that Western norms might constitute this monoculture through a process of cultural standardization (Pagano 2007: 259). Indeed, in various places in the *Working Document* the authors assert the importance of preserving regional identities and cultures in the face of cultural standardization. For example, in a discussion about cultural pluralism UNESCO (2006: 19), they comment on the fact that, in the Caribbean, what is taught in schools reflects Western paradigms rather than reflecting the regional social and cultural diversity. In the East and Pacific, it is suggested that the link between the learner and his or her society should be art education (UNESCO 2006: 46), since '[t]he arts are a living tradition through which beliefs about the environment and lifestyle are expressed.' (UNESCO 2006: 7).

It seems, then, that if the process of economic integration is to be peaceful, it must entail the recognition of cultural heterogeneity. However, the celebration of culture can be a double-edged sword because, as noted by the authors of the *Working Report*, 'culture, with its strong links to values, creed and beliefs, has the ability to both unite and divide' (UNESCO 2006: 39). Arguably, it is the problematic status of culture that renders creativity so important, since creativity is widely recognized as a universal human ability that precedes the production of culturally specific artefacts, and is posited as the fundamental building block of all human achievement (see e.g. Kaufman and Sternberg 2006). According to (Simonton 2006: 490), 'creativity made the world we live in. Remove everything about us that was not the product of the creative mind, and we would find ourselves naked in some primeval forest'.

In recognizing diverse expressions of creativity around the world, we are recognizing our common humanity and it is perhaps for this reason that the Director-General of

UNESCO declared that 'Creativity is our hope', used in the title to this chapter. In addition to providing the basis of all human civilizations, creativity is, of course, also held to be the cornerstone of our current knowledge-based economy (Jones 2003; Craft 2005) and reports such as *The Creative Age*, by Seltzer and Bentley (1999), have helped popularize the idea that the global economy is fuelled by thinking skills, and in particular by creative thinking. The idea that everyone has the ability to develop their creativity (Sternberg 1996) has likewise proved popular in the context of globalization, because this theory places value on creativity as a universal facet of human intelligence, rather than on Western knowledge. Creativity is thus presented as a Janus-faced construct that enables nations to celebrate their cultural heritage and build a prosperous future on what appears to be neutral ground.

The aim of this chapter is to explore how the message that 'Creativity is our hope' has shaped global perspectives on creativity and informed practice in primary education. In spite of the apparent global consensus on the value of creativity, there are, perhaps, as many perspectives on creativity as there are countries on earth, and it is not possible to consider all these perspectives in one chapter. Therefore, this chapter focuses on some examples of creativity research conducted in East Asia, Africa and the Arab states. These three regions have been chosen because they contain some of the fastest growing economies, some of the world's poorest economies, and some societies that are commonly thought to hold hostile views towards Western values. They are, therefore, likely to reveal a broad spectrum of thought about creativity, culture and globalization.

East Asia

Research on creativity has grown in popularity in Chinese societies in response to the rapid expansion of global economics and cultural exchange (Niu 2006: 390) and nowhere is this more evident than in Taiwan, where the Ministry of Education initiated a series of projects in 2002 aimed at making Taiwan a 'Republic of Creativity, or ROC', which is the same acronym used for the Republic of China (Niu 2006: 381). Liu's (2007) study of creativity in 99 primary schools in the Hsinchu area of Taiwan is an example of creativity research being conducted in Chinese societies which acknowledges both the local and global dimensions of creativity. Liu's (2007: 343) study was prompted by concern over 'the early appearance of creativity in young children and then the apparent decline in both interest and ability over the later elementary school years', a phenomenon that Liu (2007: 343) claims is documented internationally. Likewise, Liu's observation that it may be difficult to recognize creative children, because 'creative children may be the quirky ones who never follow directions in class, the quiet ones who never speak up in class, or the day-dreaming ones who never pay attention in class' (2007: 344), is a dilemma no doubt familiar to teachers from across the world. This study takes on a more local character when Liu notes the increased use of private art lessons for children of elementary school age in Taiwan. Thus, she suggests, makes it 'more challenging to identify those who are artistically talented students when so many have had extra lessons' (Liu 2007: 344). She suggests that this fashion may stem from the Taiwanese central government's recognition of the importance of creativity when it proclaimed, in 1996, that diversity and innovation should be the focus of modern education (Liu 2007: 344). However, the purpose of this was for the benefit of society, not the creative development of the learners.

The pragmatic goal of the Ministry of Education is shared by Liu. In her study of creativity she makes no mention of culture or 'art for art's sake', and focuses instead on the identification in the artistic expression of third-grade students of the relationship between the qualities of creativity, drawing ability, and visual and spatial intelligence (Liu 2007: 351). She found, for example, that '[s]tudents generally exhibited more original ideas in the afternoon' and proposes this as an aid to the development of 'more effective instructional practices in the regular classroom' (Liu 2007: 351). For Liu, then, creativity is a trait to be identified and developed in the primary classroom as part of performance enhancement in 'the new knowledge-based learning environment' (Liu, 2007: 344).

This study of creativity is part of a wider drive to ensure that education in Chinese societies produces a dynamic workforce that leads, rather than follows, other nations in the global economy, and this endeavour has been so successful that many people have predicted that the twenty-first century will be the 'Asian century' (Zhao 2011: viii). Although it appears that East Asian nations are re-configuring themselves in response to globalization, the traditional focus on self-cultivation in Confucian heritage cultures still derives from the Confucian belief that the primary purpose of education is to cultivate humanity, integrity, beauty, justice and equity (Li and He 2011: 4). This means that the promotion of creativity in the primary classroom is compatible with the time-honoured goals of Confucian education. This is not to say that the Confucian conception of creativity is identical to the Western conception. According to Niu (2009: 386–7), although Chinese and Western peoples recognize and agree upon many fundamental features of creativity, when judging important aspects of creativity, he states:

> Westerners tend to focus more on the individual characteristics of creative persons, such as sense of humor and aesthetic taste … [while] … Chinese people tend to focus more on the social influence of creative individuals, such as being inspirational, and contributing to the progress of society
>
> (Niu 2006: 386–7).

Kim (2009: 87) identifies the elements of Confucianism as: unconditional obedience; gender inequality; gender role expectations; and suppression of emotion. Research suggests that while Confucianism *is* negatively related to creativity in terms of self-expression, it does not appear to be detrimental to innovation nor to the technological progression of society (Kim 2009: 87). He argues that, in order to strengthen East Asian education, Confucian heritage societies need to recognize and be prepared to change the parts of the system that inhibit creativity. However, his argument is somewhat undermined by Li and He (2011: 4), who claim that the focus on the common cultural values and ethics that are deeply rooted in Confucian civilization have shaped the process of modernization and globalization in East Asia. They suggest the success of the process is due to the strength of the Confucian model of creativity, which, although somewhat different from the Western model, has provided a strong basis for knowledge-based learning.

Africa

Although Africa is widely regarded as the cradle of civilization, the formal study of creativity in Africa is of recent origin, and is bound up with efforts to modernize African economies (Mpofu *et al.* 2006: 468). For example, in January 1995, the federal government of Nigeria declared 14 September to be the National Day of Creativity to showcase national talents in the arts, sciences and technology (Mpofu *et al.* 2006: 457) and this effort to bolster national creativity underpins Sofowora's (2007) study of primary school pupils' creativity in Osun State, Nigeria. In spite of overt political support for creativity, Sofowora (2007: 913) claims that the attempt to promote creativity in Nigerian primary schools is compromised by three issues: cultural resistance to the concept of creativity; rigid adherence to the traditional 'talk and chalk' method of teaching, and chronic underfunding. These three issues are, it seems, entwined. According to Sofowora (2007: 913), in Yoruba culture, children are not allowed to ask many questions and this enforced passivity is complemented by traditional teaching methods, in which 'teachers talk and pupils listen'.

In addition, the lack of classroom facilities militates against the use of other, more innovative, methods of instruction. Notwithstanding his recognition that the average Nigerian lives on less than one dollar per day and that teachers' morale is low due to the 'deplorable condition' of school buildings and the 'non-payment of gratuity of retiring teachers' (Sofowora 2007: 919), he suggests that teachers could make use of inexpensive instructional materials and resources to invigorate their teaching (Sofowora 2007: 916). His study investigated the extent to which cartoons and comics can be used to enhance creativity in primary school pupils. Sofowora's (2007: 919) findings include the discovery that pupils were dissatisfied with the teaching strategies used by their teachers and he is highly critical of Nigerian teachers' negative attitude and reluctance to embrace what he calls 'progressive and creative' teaching. His concerns are, no doubt, justified. Both the World Bank and the United Nations have criticized the Nigerian education system, declaring that 'the quality of learning outcomes is poor and the curriculum is not appropriate for the needs of a modern society' (Johnson 2008: 47). The danger that Nigeria will never rise above 'a dollar a day' in the global economy is, therefore, real.

While East Asia has been able to drawn upon its Confucian heritage to develop a model of creativity that both answers the needs of globalization and preserves cultural heritage, many African nations have struggled to reconcile the international rhetoric of creativity with local cultures. It seems that the Western model of creativity that informs Sofowora's study is in conflict with Yoruba's culture and ways of socializing and educating children (Sofowora 2007: 913). In particular, he is critical of Yoruba taboos (e.g. concerning their religious beliefs about children who are very inquisitive and ask questions). However, according to him such taboos are slowly disappearing which is beneficial since such taboos block opportunity for creativity in young learners:

> Those that are brought up under such taboos do not have enlarged knowledge base. Hence they fear making mistakes, they do not want to be criticized and

are confused when left alone because they were not allowed to display initiative. In the Yoruba culture and in most schools in South Western Nigeria, teachers are destroying creativity in children rather than helping them grow creatively.

(Sofowora 2007: 913)

Sofowora's ideas about the Yoruba culture are, however, contradicted by Okebukola (2009), who claims that the Yoruba oral tradition is a rich source of creativity that is neither recognized nor capitalized upon in primary schools in South Western Nigeria. For example, according to Okebukola, riddle-telling at home is a rich stimulus for creativity.

Riddles in the Yoruba tradition are posed in the evenings after a day's work when people sit outside their homes to relax and narrate folk tales .... This poses a challenge to ... children as they try to outwit one another, especially when riddle telling is used for competition. This encourages creativity and critical thinking in children.

(Okebukola 2009: 317)

The marginalizing of oral traditions in Nigerian classrooms is symptomatic of the tendency to shun the use of indigenous languages in African primary schools. In an age of globalization, this practice is justified by policy makers on the grounds that 'we need English, which is a global language; indigenous languages will not get us anywhere' (Qorro 2009: 59). According to Qorro (2009: 73), the use of English (and occasionally other European languages) as the language of instruction in the classroom means that African pupils are not thinking and working in their first language. This 'constrains self-expression, self-confidence and self-advancement'. The consequence of this is that this restricts 'opportunity to question, discuss, dialogue and to think critically and creatively'. However, policy makers are not alone in favouring the use of English in African schools. Parents also seem to prefer the use of the English language for education and communication purposes (Okebukola 2009: 330). The situation is exacerbated by access to television and the internet.

Arguably, globalization has eroded faith in the educational value of cultural traditions such as riddles, songs, games and evening story-telling, which are not commonly viewed as creative (Okebukola 2009). The privileging of foreign culture and language has resulted in 90 per cent of intellectual property in Africa being stored in foreign languages, and thus being inaccessible to the African people (Qorro 2009: 73). It appears, then, that the promotion of creativity in Africa has done little to enhance equity or preserve local culture in the face of globalization.

The Arab States

In the era of globalization, the USA has attempted to extend its influence in the Middle East by setting up universities in Arab states, something El-Khairy (2010: 326) calls 'pedagogic diplomacy'. This, according to El-Khairy, is based upon the idea that

Western education will 'teach Middle Eastern youth how to deal with the Western world without forcing them into acting like Westerners or changing their personal values'. He claims that, in the post-9/11 global landscape, Middle Eastern youth has been identified as a social group that needs to be constructed as ideal 'citizen-consumers' rather than opponents of global capitalism (El-Khairy 2010: 327, 331). Policy makers have recognized that this process must be based on persuasion not coercion: in the words of US Defence Secretary, Robert Gates, 'we know we cannot kill or capture our way to victory' (Gates 2008, in El-Khairy 2010: 326).

We might, therefore, expect creativity research in the Arab region to reiterate the claims, put forward by organizations such as UNESCO, about the importance of cultural diversity and knowledge-based learning in the global economy. Instead, Al-karasneh and Saleh's (2010) study of the Islamic perspective of creativity as a model for teachers of social studies in Irbid, Jordan, explores the religious underpinnings of creativity, with minimal consideration of the economic and social demands of globalization. According to Al-karasneh and Saleh (2010: 418, 420), creativity in Islam is 'not a mere materialistic goal, but rather is a spiritual one that makes people feel strongly about the great message they are carrying in this life'. They propose that both satisfaction and happiness are 'the higher goals for creativity to be achieved in this life and in the Hereafter' (Al-karasneh and Saleh 2010: 420). Their assertion that creativity should not be about individuals *per se* but rather about social concerns (Al-karasneh and Saleh 2010: 420) is similar to the Confucian belief that the creative individual is someone who contributes to the progress of society (Niu 2006: 387). This observation raises the possibility that the Western concept of individualism, and in particular the idea of self-expression through creativity, may have limited appeal elsewhere.

At the conclusion of their study, Al-karasneh and Saleh (2010: 426) make some recommendations that include the following:

> The Ministries of Education in Muslim nations, Muslim teacher training institutions, Muslim school principals and authorities dealing with Muslim educational institutions should pay a great deal of attention towards understanding the concepts of Islamic creativity. As Muslims, they should realize that every aspect of life including practicing creativity in educational institutions, must be in accordance with Islam ... Muslim scholars who are well-versed in [the]Western view of creativity should increase their efforts in doing comparative studies between the Islamic and Western philosophy of creativity
>
> (Al-karasneh and Saleh 2010: 426).

The call for Muslims to develop an understanding of Islamic creativity, as opposed to Western creativity, is not, according to Zia (2010: 263), necessarily indicative of hostility towards non-Islamic thought. Rather, it reflects a desire to develop an 'holistic Islamic world view which is consonant and consistent with changing global contexts'. According to Zia (2010: 262), the combination of economic deprivation, the legacy of Western imperialism, and the political, social, economic, cultural and ethnic diversity of the Arab states has made it difficult for Arab people to forge an identity that might act as a bulwark against Western cultural standardization. The fragility of regional identity under globalization is documented by Fleer *et al.* (2009):

> Peterson (2005), in researching consumption and identity in Arab cultures through an analysis of Arabic children's magazines, noted that Egyptian communities are concerned for how their children can simultaneously be modern and Egyptian. He argued that a form of hybridity of cultures prevails – that is, rather than dualities of a '*galabiyya* vs. jeans and button down shirts,' 'veils vs. the salon hair style,' and 'sermon vs. TV' what is observed is 'the sheikh with a cell phone, the televised sermon, the veil, selected for color and pattern, as style accessory'
>
> (Fleer *et al.* 2009: 6)

By highlighting the divine origin of creativity, Al-karasneh and Saleh (2010) provide a platform for the development of a discourse of creativity that rises above the mundane hybridization of cultural markers, such as veils and hairstyles, and thereby enables Muslims to consolidate their culture in the face of Western cultural standardization. Furthermore, Zia (2010: 268) argues that because 'what it means to be a Muslim varies significantly across national contexts', the Western assertion that creativity is a universal facet of human intelligence can help cement the notion that Muslim people may unite under the banner of Islamic creativity.

In spite of UNESCO's assertion that 'Creativity is our hope', according to Zia (2010: 261) a concern over Islamic militancy has, she claims, 'led many politicians, religious leaders, scholars and educational professionals to raise concerns over the ways formal schooling in Muslim societies inculcates values in students'. However, in her study of the use of the Arabic language in schools in Greater Beirut, Zakharia (2009: 225) observed frequent behaviour problems in Arabic classrooms, and reported that teachers 'blamed the students and their parents for not having a sufficient appreciation for the importance of the language for Muslims and for national culture'. According to their teachers, these Lebanese pupils had 'zero culture – they and their parents. They make fun of the literary and cultural giants of our times by asking silly questions' (Zakharia 2009: 225). Far from being hotbeds of Islamic militancy, the schools visited by Zakharia were places in which cultural identity had been severely compromised by the belief that being able to speak foreign languages, and in particular English, makes individuals modern, and reduces their economic vulnerability in the global economy (Zakharia 2009: 228). She noted a stigma associated with being monolingual in Arabic because students and teachers considered it a sign that the individual was not modern or cultured.

Given that the USA wants Middle Eastern youth to be citizen-consumers of the products of global capitalism (El-Khairy 2010: 331), there is little incentive for agencies such as the World Bank to support educational initiatives that celebrate Muslim cultural identity but which are antithetical to the Western worldview, such as the development of Islamic creativity. Indeed, when the World Bank spoke out against educational provision in the Middle East and North Africa in 2008, it was with regard to its failure to support globalization, rather than its failure to support Arab culture. These territories, had not, it declared, 'capitalized fully on past investments in education, let alone developed education systems capable of meeting new challenges' (UNDP in Zaher 2010: 185).

Conclusion

Globalization is placing enormous pressure on cultures and economies around the world. Given that creativity allegedly enables individuals to both celebrate their cultural identity and develop their problem-solving abilities in the global economy, UNESCO's (2006) decision to promote creativity in education is a logical response to this pressure. However, the studies of creativity considered in this chapter suggest that the international celebration of creativity does not automatically enable individuals to transcend their local context or seize opportunities in the global economy. Where there *is* compatibility between indigenous culture and the Western rhetoric of creativity, as in Confucian heritage societies, the promotion of creativity in the primary classroom helps support knowledge-based learning. Yet, elsewhere the rhetoric of creativity has become mixed-up with the disjunction between 'old-fashioned' indigenous culture and 'modern' Western culture. As a consequence, some African nations have marginalized local culture in their primary classrooms in an attempt to embrace what is perceived as 'proper' Western creativity, while some academics in the Arab states have attempted to wrestle creativity free from the Western paradigm and define 'proper' creativity in religious terms. Clearly, then, there is something problematic about using creativity as a means of ensuring that the process of globalization is not perceived to be grossly unfair nor, indeed, violently resisted. The problem may stem from the fact that, while creativity is posited as a universal facet of human intelligence (Kaufman and Sternberg 2006), twentieth-century research into creativity was instigated in response to *Western* needs and explored in *Western* contexts (Shaheen 2010: 16). As stated previously, the Western concept of the creative person is bound up with Western individualism. Thus, in promoting creativity as a means to preserve cultural heterogeneity in the face of globalization, organizations such as UNESCO have, ironically, promoted an aspect of Western culture, and thereby augmented cultural standardization.

Branco (2009: 61) cites numerous academics who insist on the urgent need to 'investigate the socio-historical-cultural origins of individualism and competition that flourish all over the world, spread not only by the power of capitalism, but also by the associated symbolic power of values and beliefs'. In light of this statement, creativity may be viewed as something that holds symbolic power in the context of global capitalism. The chapters in this book have shown that creative thinking and problem solving have an important role to play in primary education, and no one would deny the importance of creativity and problem solving in the twenty-first century. However, it is imperative that we recognize the socio-political context of the discourse of creativity, and do not ignore the 'dormant giant' of national cultures left behind (UNESCO 2006: 7). Nor do we want to alienate or oppress people who cannot easily reconcile their cultural heritage to the perceived demands of globalization, or who do not wish to do so.

References

Al-karasneh, S.M. and Saleh, A.M. (2010) 'Islamic perspectives of creativity: a model for teachers of social studies as leaders', *Procedia Social and Behavioural Science*, 2: 412–26.

Branco, A.U. (2009) 'Cultural practices, social values and childhood education: the impact of globalisation', in M. Fleer, M. Hedegaard and J. Tudge (eds) *World Yearbook of Education 2009: Childhood Studies and the Impact of Globalisation: policies and practices at global and local levels*. Abingdon: Routledge, pp. 46–66.

Craft, A. (2005) *Creativity in Schools: tensions and dilemmas*, London: Routledge.

Dupas, G. (2001) 'The logic of globalisation: tensions and governability in contemporary society' *Management of Social Transformations – MOST Discussion Paper No. 52*, Lisbon: UNESCO. Online. Available at: http://www.unesco.org/most/dsp52.htm (accessed 5 July 2011).

El-Khairy, O. (2010) 'American dreams of reinventing the 'Orient', in A.E. Mazawi, and R.G. Sultana (eds) *World Yearbook of Education 2010: Education and the Arab 'World': political projects, struggles and geometrics of power*, Abingdon: Routledge, pp. 319–34,.

Fleer, M., Hedegaard, M. and Tudge, J. (2009) 'Constructing childhood: global–local policies and practices', in M. Fleer, M. Hedegaard and J. Tudge, (eds) *World Yearbook of Education 2009: Childhood Studies and the Impact of Globalisation: policies and practices at global and local levels*, Abingdon: Routledge, pp. 1–20.

Johnson, D. (2008) 'Improving the quality of education in Nigeria: a comparative evaluation of recent policy imperatives', pp. 45–61, in D. Johnson (ed.) *The Changing Landscape of Education in Africa: quality, equality and democracy*, Oxford: Symposium Books.

Jones, K. (2003) *Education in Britain 1944 to the Present*, Cambridge: Polity Press.

Kaufman, J.C. and Sternberg, R.J. (2006) *The International Handbook of Creativity*, New York: Cambridge University Press.

Kim, K.H. (2009) 'Cultural influence on creativity: the relationship between Asian culture (Confucianism) and creativity among Korean educators', *Journal of Creative Behaviour*, 43(2): 73–93.

Li, G.L. and He, M.F. (2011) 'A cultural overview of education in Sinic civilization', in O. Zhao (ed.) *Handbook of Asian Education: a cultural perspective*, New York: Routledge, pp. 3–6.

Liu, L.-M. (2007) 'The relationships between creativity, drawing ability, and visual/spatial intelligence: a study of Taiwan's third-grade children', *Asia Pacific Education Review*, 8(3): 343–52.

Mpofu, E., Myambo, K, Mogaji, A.A., Mashego, T.-A. and Khaleefa, O.H. (2006) 'African perspectives on creativity' societies', in J.C. Kaufman and R.J. Sternberg (eds) *The International Handbook of Creativity*. New York: Cambridge University Press, pp. 456–89.

Niu, W. (2006) 'Development of creativity research in Chinese societies', in J.C. Kaufman and R.J. Sternberg (eds) *The International Handbook of Creativity*, New York: Cambridge University Press, pp. 374–94.

Okebukola, F.O. (2009) 'Towards an enriched beginning reading programme in Yoruba', in B. Brock-Utne and I. Skattum (eds) *Languages and Education in Africa*, Oxford: Symposium Books, pp. 313–32.

Pagano, U. (2007) 'Cultural globalisation, institutional diversity and the unequal accumulation of intellectual capital', *Cambridge Journal of Economics*, 31: 649–67.

Peterson, M.A. (2005) 'The Jinn and the Computer: Consumption and Identity in Arabic Children's Magazines', *Childhood: A Global Journal of Child Research*, 12(2): 177–200.

Qorro, M.A.S. (2009) 'Parents' and policy makers' insistence on foreign languages as media education in Africa: restricting access to quality education – for whose benefit?', in B. Brock-Utne and I. Skattum (eds) *Languages and Education in Africa*, Oxford: Symposium Books, pp. 57–82.

Seltzer, K. and Bentley, T. (1999) *The Creative Age: Knowledge and skills for the new economy*, London: Demos.

Shaheen, R. (2010) 'Creativity and education' *Creative Education*, 1(3): 166–9.

Simonton, D.K. (2006) 'Creativity around the world in 80 ways … but with one destination', in J.C. Kaufman and R.J. Sternberg (eds) *The International Handbook of Creativity*. New York: Cambridge University Press, pp. 490–96.

Sofowora, O.A. (2007) 'The use of educational cartoons and comics in enhancing creativity in primary school pupils in Ile-ife, Osun State, Nigeria', *Journal of Applied Sciences Research*, 3(10): 913–20.

Sternberg, R.J. (1996) *Successful Intelligence: how practical and creative intelligence determines success in life*, New York: Simon and Schuster.

Taran, P. and Geronimi, E. (2002) 'Globalization, labor and migration: protection is paramount'. Paper presented at the *Conferencia Hemisférica sobre Migración Internacional: Derechos Humanos y Trata de Personas en las Américas, Santiago de Chile, 20–22 November*. Online. Accessible at: http://www.eclac.cl/celade/noticias/paginas/2/11302/PTaran.pdf (accessed 6 July 2011).

United Nations Educational, Scientific and Cultural Organization (UNESCO) (2006) *World Conference on Arts Education: Building Creative Capacities for the 21st Century, Lisbon, Portugal, 6–9 March*, Working Document, Lisbon: UNESCO.

Zaher, S. (2010) 'The human right to education in Arab countries: an international law perspective', in A.E. Mazawi and R.G. Sultana (eds) *World Yearbook of Education 2010: Education and the Arab 'World': Political Projects, Struggles and Geometrics of Power*, Abingdon: Routledge, pp. 183–95.

Zakharia, Z. (2009) 'Positioning Arabic in schools: language policy, national identity, and development in contemporary Lebanon', in F. Vavus and L. Bartlett (eds) *Critical Approaches to Comparative Education*, New York: Palgrave Macmillan, pp. 251–31.

Zhao, O. (2011) 'Preface', in O. Zhao (ed.) *Handbook of Asian Education: a cultural perspective*, New York: Routledge, pp. viii–xx.

Zia, R. (2010) 'Nationalism, Islamic political activism, and religious education in the Arab Region', in A.E. Mazawi and R.G. Sultana (eds) *World Yearbook of Education 2010: Education and the Arab 'World': political projects, struggles and geometrics of power*, Abingdon: Routledge, pp. 261–72.

10

Teaching for Creative Learning

Lynn Newton

We have described the nature of creativity in various subjects, some notions of creativity and some ways of supporting it in different subjects in the primary or elementary school. Creativity and problem solving are closely related [Department for Education and Employment (DfEE)/Qualifications and Curriculum Authority (QCA) 1999], although teachers may not recognize this relationship, confining the word creativity to subjects like art and music, and problem solving to subjects like mathematics and science. The previous chapters have tried to dissolve the artificial boundary. This concluding chapter is an appropriate place to bring together some of these thoughts and also add some concerns in order to provide a broader perspective for those wanting to develop creative learning across the curriculum.

Some common strands

It is interesting to note the consistency in the rankings of the subjects in terms of their perceived potential for creative thought. Both the pre-service and experienced teachers saw similar subjects as offering more or fewer opportunities for creativity than the focus subject (see Table 10.1). What is also very apparent here is the strength of the belief that creativity is synonymous with doing art, music and drama.

Notions of creativity in the different areas of the curriculum consistently reflect an arts-centred stereotype. These notions have also often been found to be relatively narrow. Opportunities for creative thought within some subjects are often seen as limited or non-existent. Even in art, music or English, the examples offered were the obvious ones – free painting, making up a tune or story writing were frequently cited as examples but the wider opportunities were rarely noted. In areas like science, and even more so in mathematics, relatively few opportunities for creative thought were suggested.

Teachers' conceptions of creativity in a subject can also be inappropriate. For instance, replicating something in design and technology or drawing a picture of an event in science may be described as creative activity. Such activities have a place in teaching and

TABLE 10.1 A comparison of views about opportunities for creative thought afforded by different subjects

Most opportunity for creative thinking

RANKING	SUBJECT(S)
1	Art
2	Drama
3	Music Design and technology English
6.5	Information and communications technology History
8	Physical education
10.5	Science Geography Religious education Modern foreign languages
13	Mathematics

Least opportunity for creative thinking

learning, but may offer little for creative thought in design and technology and science. Drawing the picture in science may be artistically creative but not scientifically creative.

Some believe that creativity is only about bringing something entirely new into the world. This means that, for example, in art, a child could not be creative because that child would be highly unlikely to produce something seen as a valuable product in the world of art. Similarly, in science, a child is unlikely to solve a problem which is of significance in the scientific world. Those with this view seem not to have considered or grasped the 'small c' concept of creativity as creating something which is new to the self. Others may place undue emphasis on certain attributes of creativity. For instance, while some novelty is a part of creative activity, it has to be appropriate novelty, often constrained by the needs of the subject or situation. Imagination rarely has free rein. So, for example, a novel explanation in science has also to be appropriate, that is, plausible.

Creativity is polymorphic in that it is expressed differently in different subjects. Nevertheless, it may draw on the same kinds of mental processes in different subjects: imagination; purposefulness; originality; and value or worth (QCA 2005). For Penny et al. (2002: 25), discussing the teaching of art and design in primary schools, creativity is inherent in the aims of subject.

Ideas are generated from visual exploration through various media, based on observation or memory. Imagination is the ability to contemplate something 'that isn't', but might be; contemplating something that currently does not exist. The imagination is developed through playful experimentation and the interplay of thoughts and handling materials.

The imagining of 'something that isn't' links very well to possibility thinking more broadly (Craft 2002) since creativity, as Tong and Palmer (2004) put it, is not just for art. For science, creativity through explanation and problem solving are also inherent in the subject's aims (Newton and Newton 2009, 2010), although this is seldom recognized.

In an exploratory study of possibility thinking with young children, Cremin, Burnard and Craft (2006) sought to determine what characterizes such thinking. They identified seven key or core elements for fostering it: posing questions; play; immersion and making connections; being imaginative; innovation; risk taking; and self-determination. They talk about the invisible pedagogy of children taking more responsibility for their learn ing journeys. However, this only works when teachers can allow pupils (and themselves) the time and space to experience the core elements and Cremin et al. (2006: 117) identify the difficulties in doing this when teachers have 'to reconcile the pressures of curriculum prescription with the demand to teach for creativity'. This point will be returned to later.

Given that fostering creativity and problem solving across the curriculum is an expectation, the concern must be that variety in teachers' notions of what counts as creative experiences for the learners could produce a very mixed response in what they offer as creative experiences, what they count as being creative and what they support in the classroom in a given subject. In effect, what one teacher does and believes to be appropriate is unlikely to be like that of another, and both could be wrong. This suggests an urgent need for teacher training institutions to include the fostering of creativity as a theme in training programmes. It also points to the inadequacy of an apprenticeship model of teacher training where the trainee learns from an experienced teacher. Such a model of skill acquisition only works where the skills concerned are soundly based and fixed and unchanging in the future. The danger is that experienced teachers will transmit inappropriate notions to trainees and perpetuate the problems. This problem needs to be recognized by those who make policy decisions about teacher training, that is, politicians and government agencies.

Some tensions

A concern for creativity in the classroom also brings with it some professional tensions. Teachers are pressed to raise standards, children are tested, and schools are ranked. A school's survival can depend on its place in the league tables. Inevitably, a teacher's attention is more on test results than on creativity. Nevertheless, teachers are urged to promote creativity in classrooms. The current preoccupation with accountability and 'performativity' shows itself strongly in the context of creative work in the classroom. Turner-Bisset (2007) analysed recent developments in primary education in the UK, particularly the prevailing climate of performativity and new initiatives on creativity. She argues that for the last 20 years, primary education has been dominated by performativity discourse and an obsession with evidence and standards. The apparent shift in government thinking to embrace the creativity discourse was reflected in a number of initiatives: the commissioning of a national report on creativity [National Advisory Committee on Creative and Cultural Education (NACCCE) 1999]; the development of the QCA report and creativity website (QCA 2005); the introduction of a Primary National Strategy [Department for Education and Skills (DfES) 2003]; government support for Creative Partnerships (a programme aimed at developing creativity in learning and participation in cultural activities (Creativity Culture and Education/Arts Council n.d.). Turner-Bisset (2007) argues that, despite such new initiatives with their focus on creativity, they have not, in fact, heralded any change in primary education and suggests that the creativity agenda has been subverted by the performativity agenda. Troman *et al.* (2007) argue for resisting the pull towards standardization and instrumentalization, something which would find favour in many Western societies.

The potential for performativity to be at odds with creativity has been noted widely. In a paper exploring and comparing the tensions between the performativity and the creativity agendas in the UK and Australian education systems, Burnard and White (2008: 669) described performativity as the numerous accountability constraints on teachers, the challenges of trying to address the outcomes of conflicting policy debates, and the requirement to meet government agendas. Consequently, teachers play safe to produce good test results and gain good appraisals. They argue for a need to re-balance pedagogy and place more trust in teacher professionalism if creative learning is to have any chance. This would then facilitate the building of collaborations and creative learning communities, able to meet any curricular requirements. They use the term 'creative pedagogy' to suggest the empowerment of teacher and learner, and the building of innovative learning cultures. In the UK, the QCA policy framework (QCA 2005) suggests that teaching for creativity (or creative learning) needs a transition from current practice and recommends that teachers re-think their pedagogy and approaches to learning and go beyond the safe and known. This tension may only be relieved if it is recognized by those who hold teachers and schools to account.

Other tensions may be relatively straightforward to resolve, stemming as they do, from teachers' everyday beliefs and misconceptions. For example, there is evidence that some teachers do not distinguish between teaching creatively and teaching for creativity. Even where teachers do recognize the difference, it is often the former rather than the latter that dominates. Indeed, Jeffrey and Craft (2004) recommend using the term creative learning, first proposed by Woods (1990), rather that teaching for creativity. They argue that distinguishing between teaching creatively and teaching for creativity could misleadingly dichotomize what should be an integrated process.

Another tension arises because some may see creativity as an addition to a curriculum and recognize neither its fundamental nature nor its existence within different subjects. Claxton *et al.* (2006: 57) argue that 'In so far as education has acknowledged creativity at all, it has focused on "allowing" rather than "developing" creativity, an arts-based "expression" rather than broader or deeper kinds of creativity; and on the role of techniques rather than dispositions'. They suggest that there is a need for cultivation of a range of habits of mind. Hartley (2006) also draws attention to the way creativity is treated as an add-on in Victoria State schools in Australia, another education system that is performance driven, standardized and monitored.

Other tensions present more of a challenge. Burns and Myhill (2004) discuss the consequences of a prescribed curriculum that has dominated many education systems in recent years. The pressures generated by such a curriculum on time limits the opportunities for creative learning. Bore (2006), following her study of creativity in science classrooms, argues that the crowded curriculum and teaching constraints, like lack of ownership of the content, restrict opportunities for creative thought. Longshaw (2009), on the other hand, argues that it would be easy to blame a prescribed curriculum for stifling creativity, as it is left to the teacher to interpret the curriculum requirements in ways which allow creative thought and activity. She suggests that the main enemy of creativity is a lack of time. She also provides examples of how, while we cannot teach creativity, we can model it, and points to the need for an environment in which children feel they can ask questions. Teachers need to be prepared to let lessons follow the children's questions. Until these problems are addressed, there may be little space for creative thinking. Although teachers may not always take control of their approach in a prescribed curriculum, they may do better if given more time and training.

Creativity can have various ends. It can, for instance, enable, empower and liberate us from helplessness. Governments, on the other hand, often prefer to point to its potential contribution to the economy. For instance, Burnard and White (2008), in a study of creativity in Australia, found it to be synonymous with *innovation* and *invention*. In the USA, Feldman and Benjamin (2006) explored the literature on the creative child in the context of early childhood education and found little systematic research focusing on education. They argue that this is because 'In the US the drive to study creativity arose from concerns about national defense and focused on technological inventiveness ...' (Feldman and Benjamin 2006: 392).

From this perspective, creativity and problem solving in, say, the clothing industry, business, and software production has more value than that which gives a personal competence or mentally richer life. But some have argued that perpetual change (resulting from creativity) is unsettling, disturbing and even disabling (McLaren 1999; Osborne 2003). The tension is that, on the one hand, a creative disposition could enable someone to lead to a self-reliant life or, used for economic purposes, produce an ever-changing worrying life. However, in the primary school, where the aim is to help children develop an enriching independence, creativity's ability to enable the individual may be paramount.

Finally, Craft (2005, 2006) discusses the cultural specificity of creativity and points out the problems of differing East–West perspectives in terms of valuing innovation as the norm. This is not to say that there is a difference between East and the West in the ability of people to be creative but there may be differences in the value, desirability and emphasis on creativity in education. Craft is also concerned that creativity can be used for good or ill so ethical considerations are also important. Her reflections lead her to the notion of fostering creativity with wisdom.

Building creative learning

No one can be creative in a vacuum. Regardless of the subject, possibility thinking draws upon skills, knowledge and understanding. Rules that constrain thought are temporarily suspended while possibilities and alternatives are considered, at times unconsciously. However, sooner or later, creative thought must be subjected to critical thought to ensure its appropriateness, plausibility or rightness of fit. Of course, what is created may be undesirable, or unethical or generally unwise. From this point of view, creative thought and action are part of a larger web of productive thought. To extract it and try to foster it in isolation is artificial and, perhaps, undesirable. Children do not simply think creatively when considering possibilities. Possibility thinking is more of an integrated than a differentiated process (Newton 2012). Moseley *et al.* (2005: 313) suggest that creative thought involves imagining situations, generating new perspectives, producing tentative explanations, planning actions and solving problems while critical thought considers its soundness and potential. Together, they offer more than each can offer alone. For this reason, it may be useful to bear in mind the broader context shown in Figure 10.1. Here we have a model for creative learning which is building on the firm

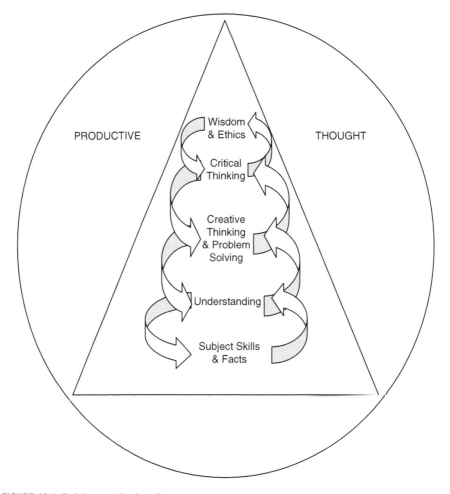

FIGURE 10.1 Building creative learning

foundations that are subject knowledge and understanding, in which creative and critical thinking are developed and used in meaningful and relevant contexts, and problem solving is encouraged and applied with wisdom.

When we think about how children learn, they do not naturally compartmentalize their ideas and understandings into subject areas. Knowledge is artificially divided into the domains we call subjects. This is a convention they learn through their schooling, a convention we, as teachers, reinforce through our planning and that governments reinforce through subject-focused curricula. Young children learn in an holistic way rather than in subject areas (see e.g. Buck *et al.* 1994). By necessity, we have discussed creativity in the context of individual subjects and offered ways to foster creative thought and action in those subject contexts. Nevertheless, some of the suggestions were cross-curricular in nature and this is an appropriate place to return to this approach.

Experienced teachers of young children will recognize the potential of play and cross-curricular themes for creativity. They present learning in a way which is relevant and meaningful to the pupils and are, therefore, more likely to capture interest and motivate. We conclude, therefore, by pointing to the potential of cross-curricular work for providing opportunities for productive thought.

For example, in the UK following the publication of *Excellence and Enjoyment* (2003), Tong and Palmer (2004) developed a creative curriculum for their school, using whole school cross-curricular themes like *The Sea*. They found several positive outcomes from this experience, including that teaching for creativity helped to motivate the children and encourage them to become independent learners. Similarly, in the USA, Maker *et al.* (2008) describe encouraging creativity through a project called DISCOVER (Discovering Intellectual Strengths and Capabilities while Observing Varied Ethnic Responses). The team created a cross-curricular model which required problem solving for use with elementary school children and which could underpin the development of intelligence (or more specifically, giftedness) and creativity. They provide examples of problems from the programme that reflect varying degrees of structure for students in different elementary school grades. For example, at Grade 2 (8–9 years) the content related to the theme of *Cycles*. Observation of the classroom while the pupils were working indicated a number of characteristics of the lessons that might encourage creative and productive thinking and problem solving:

- the experiences involved freedom of choice;
- the pupils set their own goals and decided how to meet them;
- there was open discussion of possibilities;
- a challenge was provided (to create something);
- pupils had the opportunity to work independently or collaboratively;
- probing questions from the teacher encouraged explanation and justification;
- pupils helped define clear expectations of the outcome; and
- a presentation of the products was made in which pupils interacted with each other.

For children to exercise their imagination in this way in any subject and develop their creative thinking and problem-solving abilities, there needs to be a sound knowledge base. In many countries, the teachers of elementary or primary age children teach across a broad curriculum, unlike their secondary colleagues who specialize in one or two subjects only. The onus is on elementary or primary school teachers to know not only the subject content but also what counts as productive thought in the different areas of the curriculum (Newton 2012). They also need to know how they can support the construction of understanding, the strategies and approaches that will scaffold the learning with understanding. This cross-curricular approach adds to a teacher's repertoire of ways of fostering productive thought more generally.

If we really want teachers to foster creativity and problem solving in their classrooms, they will need to know what it means, be aware of the tensions, and have ways to achieve their goals.

References

Bore, A. (2006) 'Bottom-up for creativity in science? A collaborative model for curriculum and professional development', *Journal of Education for Teaching*, 32(4): 413–22.

Buck, M., Inman, S. and Moorse, K. (1994) *Educating the Whole Child: Cross-curricular themes within the history curriculum*, Occasional Paper 10, London: Historical Association.

Burnard, P. and White, J. (2008) 'Creativity and performativity: counterpoints in British and Australian education', *British Educational Research Journal*, 34(5): 667–82.

Burns, C. and Myhill, D. (2004) 'Interactive or inactive? A consideration of the nature of interaction in whole class teaching', *Cambridge Journal of Education*, 34(1): 35–49.

Claxton, G., Edwards, L.and Scale-Constantinou, V. (2006) 'Cultivating creative mentalities: A framework for education', *Thinking Skills and Creativity*, 1: 57–61.

Craft, A. (2002) *Creativity and Early Years Education*, London: Continuum.

Craft, A. (2005) *Creativity in Schools: Tensions and Dilemmas*, London: RoutledgeFalmer

Craft, A. (2006) 'Fostering creativity with wisdom', *Cambridge Journal of Education*, 36(3): 337–50.

Creativity Culture and Education (CCE)/Arts Council England (n.d.) *Creative Partnerships: changing young lives*, Newcastle: CCE Publication. Online. Available at: http://www.creativecultureeducation.org (accessed November 2010).

Cremin, T., Burnard, P. and Craft, A. (2006) 'Pedagogy and possibility thinking in the early years', *Thinking Skills and Creativity*, 1: 108–19.

Department for Education and Skills (DfES) (2003) *Excellence and Enjoyment: a strategy for primary schools*, Nottingham: DfES Publications Centre.

Department for Education and Employment/Qualifications and Curriculum Authority (DfEE/QCA) (1999) *The National Curriculum Handbook for Primary Teachers in England Key Stages 1 and 2*, London: DfEE/QCA.

Feldman, D.H. and Benjamin, A.C. (2006) 'Creativity and education: an American retrospective', *Cambridge Journal of Education*, 36(3): 319–36.

Hartley, D. (2006) 'The instrumentalization of the expressive in education', in A. Moore (ed.) *Schooling, Society and Curriculum*, London: Routledge, pp. 60–70.

Jeffrey, B. and Craft, A. (2004) 'Teaching creatively and teaching for creativity: distinctions and relationships', *Educational Studies*, 30(1): 77–87.

Longshaw, S. (2009) 'Creativity in science teaching', *School Science Review*, March, 90(332): 91–4.

Maker, C.J., Sonmi, J. and Muammar, O.M. (2008) 'Development of creativity', *Learning and Individual Differences*, 18: 402–17.

McLaren, R.B. (1999) 'Dark side of creativity', in M.A. Runco and S.R. Pritzker (eds) *Encyclopedia of Creativity*, San Diego: Academic Press.

Moseley, D., Baumfield, V., Elliott, J., Gregson, M., Higgins, S., Miller, J. and Newton, D.P. (2005) *Frameworks for Thinking*, Cambridge: Cambridge University Press.

National Advisory Committee on Creative and Cultural Education (NACCCE) (1999) *All Our Futures: creativity, culture and education*, London: Department for Education and Employment.

Newton, D.P. (2012) *Teaching for Understanding: What it is and how to do it*, 2nd edn, London: Routledge.

Newton, D.P. and Newton, L.D. (2009) 'Some student teachers' conceptions of creativity in school science', *Research in Science and Technological Education*, 27(1): 45–60.

Newton, L.D. and Newton, D.P. (2010) 'Creative thinking and teaching for creativity in elementary school science', *Gifted and Talented International*, 25(3): 111–23.

Osborne, T. (2003) 'Against "creativity": a philistine rant', *Economy and Society*, 32(4): 507–25.

Penny, S., Ford, R., Price, L. and Young, S. (2002) *Teaching Arts in Primary Schools*, Exeter: Learning Matters.

Qualifications and Curriculum Authority (QCA) (2005) *Creativity: find it, promote it! – promoting pupils' creative thinking and behaviour across the curriculum at key stages 1, 2 and 3 – practical materials for schools*, London: QCA.

Tong, A. and Palmer, C. (2004) 'Creativity – it's not just for art', *Teacher to Teacher – Primary and Pre-School*, Autumn 2004: 8–9.

Troman, G., Jeffrey, B. and Raggl, A. (2007) 'Creativity and performativity policies in primary school cultures', *Journal of Education Policy*, 22(5): 549–72.

Turner-Bisset, R. (2007) 'Performativity by stealth: a critique of recent initiatives on creativity', *Education 3–13*, 35(2): 193–203.

Woods, P. (1990) *Teacher Skills and Strategies*, London: Falmer.

Index